Stop Living In This Land
Go To The Everlasting World
Of Happiness
Live There Forever

Stop Living In This Land
Go To The Everlasting World Of Happiness
Live There Forever
by Woo Myung

First Edition
First Printing Mar. 2012
Second Printing Sep. 2012

Published by Cham Books
50 Massachusetts Ave. Arlington MA 02474 U.S.A.
Tel: 6172726358
chambooks.inc@maum.org

ISBN: 978-0-9849124-0-7

Library of Congress Control Number: 2011963362

This book has been translated into English from the original Korean text.
Translated by members of the Maum Meditation Translation Team.

All creative work, illustrations and calligraphy (covered under copyright) are by the author.

Book Design by Color of Dream

Printed in Seoul, Korea

Stop Living In This Land
Go To The Everlasting World
Of Happiness
Live There Forever

Woo Myung

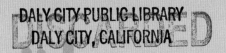

S

Woo Myung, bestselling author of many books about Truth, attained enlightenment after deep introspection about life and existence. When he became Truth, he dedicated his life to teaching others to become Truth and founded Maum Meditation. For his efforts, he was awarded the Mahatma Gandhi Peace Award by the United Nations International Association of Educators for World Peace (IAEWP) in September 2002. Woo Myung has also been appointed as a United Nations World Peace Ambassador.

He is the author of numerous books including *Nature's Flow*, *World Beyond World*, *Where You Become True Is The Place Of Truth* and *The Way To Become A Person In Heaven While Living* which have been published in English. His other books, *Heaven's Formula For Saving The World*, *The Living Eternal World*, *The Book Of Wisdom*, *Mind* and *The Enlightened World* are in the process of being translated into English as well as Chinese, French, German, Italian, Japanese, Portuguese, Spanish and Swedish.

Contents

Part 2 The Human Mind

Part 3 God's World Beyond The Human World

Part 4 The Everlasting World

Part 5 The Living Empty Sky

While travelling around the world, I have found that although the languages and customs of each place are different, people's lives are essentially the same - everyone eats and tries to subsist. However, no one knows where it is that they are going, what they live for, or why they live and die. These are questions man cannot solve, if he even contemplates them at all.

I have attended many meetings around the world, with U.N. members and spiritual, religious and political leaders, as well as holding seminars, discussions and giving speeches for people worldwide. Regardless of the location or audience, my message has always been the following:

It is because man is incomplete that religions have been split into countless different denominations, and the reason there are many different political ideologies is that such thoughts and systems arise from man's incomplete mind. I tell them that when man becomes complete, he will transcend religion, and all schools of thought, politics, philosophy and education will go beyond what exists at present and become Truth - they will become complete. I tell them that it will thus become possible for the world to become a place where all are one. This can happen when people change from their human minds to the mind of the Universe, the mind of Truth, and are created anew in the Universe. They are then complete because they are immortal and without death. When the above is explained in this way, all people agree.

From an age when people stored false and futile things in their minds, it has now become the age when man can live forever by discarding the minds he has put in his mind, thereby becoming the mind of the Universe and being reborn.

I also tell them that everyone in the world will become complete because Maum Meditation has the method for human completion. If people get rid of their false minds, they will be born as Truth with true minds, so it will be possible for everybody to become one.

People ask me if this is possible in reality, to which I tell them it has already been realized and that many people have already become complete. When people cast off their heavy burdens, not only do they become healthier because they are no longer stressed, they become saints. It is currently an age when anyone can become a saint.

Everyone agrees when they are told that to achieve this, man must go from adding to his mind, which was indicative of the age of incompletion, to subtracting what is in his mind, and he will then become the original mind which is Truth and the Universe. They applaud when I tell them that once a person is reborn from this Universe, this place here is the complete world that does not die; that right here is everlasting heaven. Many people begin the practice of discarding their minds after hearing this.

It is possible to know all the ways of the world when one is free from his illusionary, individual mind and sees with the mind of the Universe. Furthermore, when one is reborn with the everlasting body and mind of the Universe, he can escape death and live forever.

If until now, the history of mankind has been one of rapid development of a material civilization, then it is now the age of a new world - a world of the true consciousness that unfolds on this land wherein this place here is heaven while we are living. That time is now.

Throughout history we only heard of Truth, but it is now the age when anyone can become a saint and a holy person. What people truly need to do is to become Truth and complete, and thus become immortal. There is nothing more important in the world than living, which is why there can be nothing more important than this.

Part 1

The Reason We Are Born
And Why We Live

Now is the time, now, when God, Buddha, great compassion and love
come to the world and take man who would otherwise disappear to
the living land of Truth; when man can have the mind of God and be
reborn in the mind of God by cleansing his mind; when man can be
saved. Is there anything in the world more important than this? This
is the reason man comes into the world.

From Despair To Hope

There were people living in the world even a long time ago. The many people who lived in the world throughout the ages have all disappeared, silently and without a trace. While they lived, they were attached to the realities of their daily lives and they suffered because of their minds of possession, but despite all of their agonizing over the meaningless events of life, no trace of them remains. Ultimately, there is no meaning in human life.

The only way for man to live forever and escape from suffering and burden is to die while he is still living. Only then can he find his true self. His true self is God who remains when he is dead.

Even if all people and the world disappear, what remains is the existence without form, taste, scent, sight, hearing and feeling. That is, the existence - for which these minds have completely ceased - remains: the original foundation. If one is reborn from the original foundation, he and the world become eternal and never-dying immortals, and both the world and man live, for they become God that never dies.

Discarding falseness and becoming real is the only path to life. People want to become real but at the same time keep the falseness; there are not many people who know that they can only become real if they throw away what is false. They have such strong attachments to their falseness that they look for Truth within it. They do not know that Truth does not exist within falseness - that is how foolish people are. The right way, or the answer, is to discard falseness so that only Truth remains, and to be reborn as Truth.

Enlightenment

In the world there are falseness and Truth. Man's mind that lives copying what belongs to the world is false, and the world is true. Man is not one with the mind of the world; instead he lives in an overlapping copy of it. In any case, it is a certain fact that he lives in his own mind world. He comes to know Truth to the extent that the mind of the world enters his, and this is enlightenment.

Man's mind is made up of illusionary pictures. Consequently, when he throws away these pictures Truth will enter into his mind, and he will know Truth to the extent of what he has discarded. This is enlightenment. Only when one repents, can one gain enlightenment and go to the place of Truth. It is the same principle as washing dirty clothes - the more you clean the dirt away, the more it goes back to its original state. A piece of paper, which has been scribbled on, gets cleaner the more the scribbling is erased. Enlightenment is the same as knowing the true state of the paper once it is clean.

To Know The World Is One

There is one world, but it is seen in millions of different ways because there are millions of different human minds. Born as the child, the offspring, of incomplete people, man takes pictures of things in the complete world through his eyes, nose, ears, mouth and body, and stores them inside his mind.

This mind world, which overlaps the real world, is man-made and a duplicate. Inside this illusionary world, man lives making ever more illusions. The Bible tells us, "blessed are the poor in spirit, for theirs is the kingdom of heaven", which means heaven that is the true world will become one's own when he discards his false mind completely.

The phrase "cleanse or empty one's mind" means one should discard and destroy this false mind, which has turned its back on the origin and is an enemy of the world. Because this mind is egotistical, narrow-minded and self-centered, it has discriminations, judgments of right and wrong, likes and dislikes, life and death, enemies and lovers, and distinctions between what does and does not belong to it. Because pictures, the false mind, live as the master, man is born as the child of falseness, lives in a world of falseness and then passes on to a non-existing false world. It is the reason he ends up dying.

For man to become complete he must discard the false world; he must discard the Earth, moon, stars and sun of this world; and he must discard even the materials in the air. What then remains is the place of the Creator, God and Buddha. This place is the origin, and from this viewpoint it is always this place, the original foundation, regardless of whether the creations of the world exist.

From man's perspective however, the world is a place with countless different things because his mind is not one with the world. When the world is seen from the place of the origin and source, it is one. It is one when nothing in the world exists, and even when they do exist, it is still one. Only a person who has returned to the origin and become the true mind can know this.

The Age Of Nature's Flow

The life of nature's flow, or universal order, is a life of great nature and a life of Truth. Nature's flow is when there is no forcedness or stubbornness. It is a life that is lived according to the way things happen, which is possible when these minds do not exist. It is often thought that living life in this way is being complacent but it is actually a life of diligent action without blockages or strife. When one can live his life in this way, it means that his mind has become the mind of nature.

Nature, namely this world, provides us with oxygen, water, and all that we need, yet it has no mind of having given us these things. True love and affection is when, like nature, one lives for the people of the world without the mind that he does so. It is when one lives with the mind of nature. True love and affection is to give without expectations, just as the world, as nature, gives.

How free would people be, if they could live like this! There would be no conflicts or blockages in their minds; people would be able to trust each other and love others more than they love themselves. When people's minds become the mind of God and when all people live a life of nature's flow, it will be a world worth living in!

Now is the time of human completion, the age of nature's flow, and it is the time for the world to become one. It is a time when everyone can become the mind of God, of one mind, the righteous mind. It is the time to live a life of nature's flow. This is what is meant by the age of nature's flow.

The Reason Man Is Born Into This World

An innumerable number of people have come and gone in this world, but no one knows where they came from or where they went. In any case, they have all disappeared from the world. From the Universe's point of view, man disappears after a fleeting, meaningless life; there is little difference between a mayfly that passes away after a day and man who passes away after seventy to eighty years. Only man dies holding onto all the events and stories from his life. If he looks back on those stories after time has passed, he would realize that it is all meaningless.

When the Creator created man, he was made to resemble him. However, man made his own self-centered world by copying what is in the Creator's world. He lost his original nature and began to lead a selfish life, but it enabled civilization to progress; man's greed enabled the population of the world to multiply rapidly and without it, mankind would have died out naturally. The Creator will come to the world to save mankind at a time in the world when it is populated to capacity. Human life, like the life of a mayfly, is meaningless, yet at the same time it is the will of the Creator to "harvest" man when the human population is at its densest - that is, it is the Creator's will to save people when there are as many people living in the world as possible. Now is the time of that harvest. We should live forever in the land of God by becoming one with the mind of God instead of dying meaninglessly with resentments and regrets. The reason and purpose man is born into the world is to live forever.

To all people, who disappear like smoke, without meaning: Just once, think deeply about yourself so that we may go together to live in the world that is eternally alive. There is no meaning in human life; nothing remains from it and everything from it disappears. Now is the time, now, when God, Buddha, great compassion and love come to the world and take man who would otherwise disappear to the living land of Truth; when man can have the mind of God and be reborn in the mind of God by cleansing his mind; when man can be saved. Is there anything in the world more important than this? This is the reason man comes into the world.

From The Time Man Was Born In The World And Has Lived On The Earth

Since mankind was created in the world, people lived their lives continuously forming and destroying delusional thoughts and notions in order to possess and own more.

There have always been mythical stories of a world different from this one - a land of peace where everyone can live a good life. However these stories were told abstractly and conceptually and there was no one who actually knew this world. Countless people devoted their precious youth in searching for this world, and innumerable others sought it in religion, but no one was able to find it.

Past saints and sages spoke as if this world had already been fulfilled, but they were empty words because if it had been, a method of fulfillment would exist. Such a method has never existed, so aren't their words simply empty boasts?

How many people failed to achieve this end, and spent their lives sighing in a dark world? A method to achieve it did not exist because a person who had achieved it did not exist. The past was an age of simply talking about Truth; all religions and people who claimed to have achieved this world were only talking about Truth. The age of talking about Truth is over, and now it is the age of becoming Truth. The past was an age of adding to one's illusionary mind. Now it is the age of subtraction.

To Be Alive

Man believes that what is in the world is alive and what is not in the world or what has disappeared, is dead. In fact, it is people, humans, who are dead. Man is dead because he is not one with the eternal mind of the world. He is trapped inside his own mind, within his preconceptions and habits, formed by taking pictures of countless things from his illusionary mind world.

Man continuously makes illusions by putting the world and all that happens in the world inside him. His thoughts, his very ways of thinking, are wrong because he lives inside these illusions. Therefore, his thought that he is alive is also wrong. Anything in the world that is seen from man's perspective is wrong. When one sees from the perspective of the world, the perspective of Truth, he can know that when people die, they die forever. One must be born in the world of Truth in order to become a person who is alive - a person who does not die.

Being alive means one has been born in the true world, and being dead means one does not exist in the true world.

What God Is

Even though we are always with God, a person who lives within the false human mind only has what is within his illusionary false mind. Man does not know God because God's mind does not exist within the human mind. In the world that is true, God is both everything in existence and the emptiness where there is nothing, but man cannot see or know God because he lives not in the world but in a copy of the world.

Everything in the world is God. God, the Creator and the origin is the place before all of creation, where all material forms in the Universe have been taken away. The existence in this place is *Jung* and *Shin*, namely the Soul and Spirit, and this existence is God.

This existence exists of and by itself whether or not creation exists; it exists before and after the beginning, of and by itself, and it is the existence of God. As this existence is metaphysical, a non-material entity, only those who have become the mind of this existence itself can see and know it.

God is the master and owner of all creations, and everything in creation is God and the children of God. When this existence comes as a human-being, all creations can be born in the land of God and live forever - this is heaven. God is alive but his is the place beyond human preconceptions and habits.

Creation I

There are two types of creation: material creation and spiritual creation.

The way all of the many different forms in the world came into existence was by the right set of conditions for creation coming together. This type of creation is called material creation. Material creation is possible because the celestial bodies in the sky exist, and soil, water, wind, and temperature exist on Earth. From the perspective of the Universe, the Creator, it is the Creator who created all things.

Everything in the world comes from the origin that is the Creator, and when material substances cease to exist they return to the origin. This is the law of nature. However when the time of nature's harvest comes, as it surely will, the Creator will enable everything to be reborn as the Soul and Spirit of the Universe. Man can live as this existence of Truth when he has been given new birth in the land of this original existence. Such a time is the age of discarding falseness and becoming Truth. This kind of creation is spiritual creation; the creation of the Soul and Spirit.

The Definition Of Truth

Truth is an everlasting, never-changing and living existence. This is the correct definition of Truth. The existence that is everlasting, never-changing and alive is the body, *Jung*, and mind, *Shin*, of the Universe, which existed before the great Universe. This existence is the sky before sky: the emptiness that is the great Universe itself. It is Truth and the very Soul and Spirit of the great Universe.

It is a metaphysical entity that exists, of and by itself, in all creations. It is the source and the origin of all things. It does not exist yet it does exist; although it exists, it has no form. It cannot be seen or known by the human mind; it is only possible to know this existence when one's mind goes beyond his human mind and becomes one with this existence. If one is reborn as the Soul and Spirit of this existence, he is Truth and can live forever without death. This existence exists, as the Universe itself. Regardless of the countless creations that come and go it just exists, as the body and mind of the never-dying immortal origin. This existence is Truth. Unless one's Soul and Spirit is reborn in the land of this existence, nothing is eternal. Being reborn as the Soul and Spirit, in the land of the Soul and Spirit - the origin of all material form - is the completion of the Universe. This is what is meant by becoming Truth.

Do You Know Where You Will Go When You Pass On To The Afterworld?

From long ago, many people have spoken of the afterworld. In Buddhism, it is said that the afterworld one goes to is determined by one's relationships and karma; that those who do good deeds will go to paradise, while those who do not will go to hell. Christianity tells us that those who do good deeds and believe in Jesus Christ will go to heaven whereas those who are evil and do not believe in Jesus Christ will go to hell.

I have been to several funerals and at each funeral, the rites were carried out according to the deceased's religious beliefs. However I found that no one truly knew where their beloved had gone. When the topic of the afterworld comes up in funerals or during general daily conversations, those with religious beliefs speak in keeping with what they had learned through their religious scriptures while others who are non-religious believe that one simply disappears after death.

If we had a better understanding of man, we would be able to easily know the answer. The moment we humans are born into this world we take pictures of the world and of our whole lives: pictures of everything we do, our families, enemies, money, love, fame, and everything in our lives. This is what people do. Because the real world and man's individual mind world overlap, he does not know that he is living in his mind world, and mistakenly believes himself to be living in the real world. However, he is not of the real world; he is a person of his own mind world. He is always trying to appease his feelings of inferiority and from within his mind, he loves, hates, has inner conflicts, likes and dislikes. However these are all just his own minds. The human mind world is false; it is a non-existent delusional world. When a person who is within his mind world dies, he dies forever in it. In other words, he follows his ties, his relationships and the karma that he has accrued, but this afterworld he goes to is a delusional world which does not exist in the real world. It is hell.

The law of the world is that all material existences in the world come from the origin that is Truth and return to it. But people on the other hand, all go to the mind worlds they have made and die forever. True life is returning to and being reborn in the origin that is the Creator and Truth by destroying one's mind world. This is heaven, and only then can one live forever. Man dies unless he repents because no one in the world is righteous - he ends up becoming a dream that does not exist in the true world. Only one whose Soul and Spirit of Truth, the origin of the world, has been born will live. People end up dying because they do not have the Soul and Spirit of the world. He whose true Soul and Spirit is resurrected by repenting and going to Truth, the original foundation, will live forever.

How Can You Die While Living Without Your Body Dying?

The Universe that is devoid of any material things existed before you were born and it exists whether you are born or not. Having forsaken this existence - the Universe, which is your origin and master - you are living in your own mind world that is not the mind of this existence and your whole life is the life of a dream. If you throw away the life lived in a dream and yourself inside the dream, then you will disappear - this is death. Death is when you are gone and only the origin remains. Death is the disappearance of man's self and his sins and karma, thereby allowing him to return to the origin while he is living.

One can die completely only when the body is living; if the body dies then he really dies. Therefore, one must die and be reborn while he is alive. Death means one's false self does not exist. If one truly dies, then he goes to the place of Truth and is reborn. He accomplishes human completion and becomes God. One's body and mind can die completely only when he is alive.

The Dead Are The Living And The Living Are The Dead

People believe they are alive and those who are religious also believe that they will go to heaven after they die. However, man is not living in God's world but in the mind world he has made. This is because it is human nature to live in a world that has copied God's world, a counterfeit world that resembles God.

He has betrayed God by making his own world. The world man has made does not exist in God's world. His world is the enemy of God; one that has turned away from God. This is the reason man is a sinner. From the perspective of the origin, the true God, it is a non-existent world that only exists in one's own mind - an illusion. It is a world where one thinks according to the false minds contained in his own mind world.

Man is an entity that does not exist; he is incomplete. Even though many people have spent their precious youth and lives seeking Truth through religion and other means, they have been unable to find Truth because what is incomplete can only find incompletion.

Many things have existed in the world but all that had existed have disappeared, as will the Earth one day. They came from the origin and have gone back to the origin. This is the way of the world. Man however, does not know this; he lives in his own non-existent dream world and without being able to go back to the origin, he dies in vain and disappears.

One's mind world is a non-existent picture world. Therefore, it does not exist in the world. Everyone living in the picture world has disappeared. Life in the picture world disobeying God and Truth is hell. It is hell because it is the same as living inside a picture or a video. Just like a dream, it does not exist after you wake up.

It is a world made of pictures that man has taken during his life, through his eyes, nose, mouth, ears and body. From the perspective of the Universe, the origin, human life is a dream that lasts a split second and it does not exist in the Universe. This is why people in the olden days compared life to a dream or a bubble that is worthless, short, and futile.

If one discards and kills his self, and is ashamed and remorseful to heaven for his false world and his self living in it, heaven will become his and he will be born in that land and live there.

The dead are the living, because he who tries to die lives. But those who try to live are dead, because they are not Truth; they are false.

Falseness And Reality

Falseness is what does not exist and reality is what does exist. The human mind world that man makes is false and the world is real. It is the way of the world that everything in the world comes from and returns to the origin, the source, or the original foundation.

The origin is the only thing that is real. People are dead and false because they take pictures of the real world and live inside those pictures. Everything in the world came from the original foundation and is the original foundation whether it exists or not. Only the original foundation is real.

Moreover, when everything in the world has been born in the true world which is the original foundation, it will all become real, eternal and without death. Only what is real is alive and what is false is dead and does not exist.

People Do Not Know How To Receive Jesus

Man is waiting for the coming of a delusional Truth; an existence made from his own beliefs and standards. Man believes this entity of Truth will come only for him and he waits for this entity in order to gain something; he believes that a Jesus of love and benevolence will come only to save him. He believes this because he lives within his own self-made mind world.

Jesus is the existence of Truth. A person who has become one with the Creator that is God - a person whose Soul and Spirit is born in the land of the Creator - is this existence. I asked people if they could accept into their home a Jesus who is homeless and a beggar; one who lived under a bridge, and had boils, head lice, layers upon layers of dirt on his body and incurable contagious diseases. Could they bring him home, bathe him, tend to his diseases and obey his wishes? It was clear that no one could readily do so.

Just as it says in the Bible, your mind can become one with Jesus and you can receive him only when you give up your spouse, children and fortune. This is true belief. However, man has a selfish and self-centered mind and lives only for himself. True love, or great compassion, is making man discard the preconceptions and habits from his false human mind world and change falseness into Truth so that he can go to the land of Truth. Man, who is false, mistakenly believes that Jesus will take him to heaven just as he is, but isn't it illogical to believe one can go to heaven while retaining all of his falseness?

Without a doubt, the existence of Truth, Jesus, would tell man who is false to wash away his sins - his false images - and tell him to discard all of his fixed preconceptions and habits. By making him do all the things that he dislikes the most and forbidding him from doing what he likes, Jesus will change man's mind into the mind of God. Because his word is law, man must die when he is asked to die and he must discard when he is asked to discard. Man must not do what he is told not to do. When he discards everything and his mind transcends all things, he will be able to become the mind of God.

At the age of thirty-three, Jesus questioned why God had abandoned him, yet he accepted his death by saying, "...not as I will, but as you will." By accepting his death Jesus received God in his mind and became the mind of God. Likewise, only one who loves righteousness more than himself can go to heaven. Ask yourself whether you can die right now for righteousness as Jesus did. One who cannot do this will end up dying. He will die because his Soul and Spirit of righteousness has not been born, and he does not have the kingdom of righteousness within.

One Must Repent To God - The True Mind - That Is Within Him

The reason we repent is so that we can go from our false worlds to the true world and be reborn there. We repent so that we can discard our minds that are false and become the true mind. It is also in order to discard ourselves that are sinners and become our true selves.

One's sins are the falseness in his mind. Therefore, when one discards the falseness within himself, he is discarding his sins. One must throw away the images inside his mind until only Truth remains. One must repent to God, the true mind, until all of his sins have disappeared.

A ghost is still a ghost even if it repents. This is because it repents from within the ghost world - from within the ghost's mind. When one repents from inside his human mind instead of repenting to God, it remains in his mind as a delusion. Because he has this delusion in his mind, it eventually begets more delusions. When these delusions form into action, he will commit countless transgressions.

When people who are false, illusions and ghosts "repent" together, it makes the participators collective ghosts. They become members of a ghost "gang" in their minds. In medical terms this is called joint megalomania. If the host of this condition is false, his delusions will continue in an endless stream of falseness, so all those who have entered into his collective megalomania will end up in this "gang" forever. There is nothing more dangerous in the world than this, where people end up crazy - patients of collective megalomania. Out of touch with reality, they are demented without knowing that they are so and they end up doing harm to society.

Where Is Heaven?

Many people think about death and have questions about it but there is no one who knows the answers to their questions. Each religion talks of a world beyond this world: in Buddhism, it is said the world of paradise, where Buddha resides, exists. In Christianity, it is said that heaven exists. However, no one knows which place is true.

In any case, heaven is a world that exists and hell is a world that does not exist. Man is born into the world with a limited amount of time. During his time in the world, he stands at a crossroads of living or dying. However, no one in the world truly realizes this. No one knows whether he will die or live, because man does not have true knowledge that comes from wisdom.

There have been billions of people on Earth who lived seventy to eighty years and passed away. While many people believe they moved on to another place, the only thing that is certain is that they have disappeared from this world.

The principle of the world is that you exist because the ground exists; the ground exists because the Earth or the foundation exists; the Earth, sun, moon and stars in the sky exist because the empty Universe exists. This is the origin or the original foundation. This original foundation is the master of the Universe and only this original foundation is Truth.

For us, people, our lives in this world are the same as dreaming a mere dream. From the perspective of the everlasting existence, Truth, which has existed since the beginning, we are dreaming a dream that lasts only for a split-second.

The original foundation or the place beyond material existence is Truth, the master of the Universe and the Creator. This existence is a non-material, immortal and living existence; it is the master of the world; it is the *Jung* and *Shin* of the Universe that is the master of the world; the Universe's Soul and Spirit. The only eternal existence in the Universe is this existence. For man to live forever he must be reborn with the Soul and Spirit, or the body and mind, of this existence. Otherwise, there is no such thing as eternity in the world.

The human mind is the mind of sin and karma; a false mind world which has copied what belongs to the real world. What is in the world is true but man lives not in the world but inside his own mind which is like a video. This world is hell; an illusionary world. It is false and it does not exist in the real world. From the viewpoint of the real world, it does not exist. In other words, the illusionary world of the video does not exist in the world.

Since man does not live in the world and instead lives in his mind - a copy of the world that overlaps with the world - when he dies he simply disappears. However, when he erases his self-made mind world which is false, the original foundation remains.

If we think about it, the original foundation existed before you were born and it exists now. It will still exist even after you die. Unless you swap your mind to this existence of Truth, which is the origin, an eternal land does not exist. Doesn't the Universe still exist even after both your mind world and yourself disappear? Material matter in the Universe exists because your mind exists; even after all material matter is erased, the sky still exists. When you become this empty sky and you are reborn from this sky, you will never die.

Only this place is the land without death and this land is a world where one lives forever. If man discards his mind world and his self living in it, he will have the mind of the origin and if his mind becomes this mind of the origin, his mind will become the mind of the world. Within this mind of the world, one's true soul that is the substance of Truth must be reborn. Only then can his body and mind of the true soul live forever in this world even after the body disappears.

It is here that heaven exists. God or Buddha exists in the mind of a person who has become one with the mind of the world, and it is here that heaven also exists. He who has become this mind has the mind of the world. He will live forever in this land, in the world of the Soul and Spirit, where everything in this world is as it is.

Because it is said that we will live with this body in this land, some people and some religions believe that it is the physical body that will live forever. However it is Truth and the principle of nature that man's physical body cannot live forever. As scientists have proven, even the stars in the sky, including the Earth, have life spans and can only live up to fifteen billion years. It is not the material form that lives, but the original foundation, the Soul and Spirit which is Truth, which will live forever here in this land of Truth. Such a place is heaven. To be reborn and to live in this heaven, one must discard his mind of sins and karma that has turned its back on the world. He must become the mind of the world and within that mind, the world and one's self must be resurrected as the Soul and Spirit, in order to live in this land which is heaven.

Creation II

There are two types of creation: spiritual and material. The Creator that is the master of the world is not a material existence but a metaphysical one. It is the origin and source of the Universe; it is the Universe before the Universe. This existence is *Jung* and *Shin* (Soul and Spirit). Amidst absolute nothingness, *Jung* and *Shin* exists; *Jung* is the place of emptiness and *Shin* is God that exists in the emptiness. All physical forms in the world are representations of this existence.

The creation of the world happened when this existence, of and by itself, came forth when the conditions were right. The material world was created by itself according to the right set of circumstances. Everything here in this world exists because the sky, the Earth, and the celestial bodies exist. All these things are created by the omnipotent Creator, according to the conditions of the environment; they are the representations and the children of the Creator. The Creator's shape and form is the existing world, thus it is omnipotent.

It is the way of the world, and Truth, that everything comes from and returns to the Creator. Becoming one with the Creator is spiritual creation. The soul of one who is reborn as *Jung* and *Shin*, which is the substance of the Creator, is Truth and does not die. Spiritual and material creation can only be done by the Creator because the Creator is the master, and only the master has the ability to create.

The Creator, the source, created the material. Spiritual creation is when the Creator, in human form, saves the world in the land of *Jung* and *Shin* and takes man to this land. When the Creator is in one's mind, and the land of Truth and the Creator is also in one's mind, he has become one with the Creator and can then be reborn with the Creator's Soul and Spirit. Only the Creator can create. The Creator can give salvation because he enables the world to be reborn and live in the land of the Creator.

Man Does Not Live In The World, He Is Not True But False So He Is Dead

From the beginning, the world was created complete; it is already enlightened and has life. Because man is not born in this world, he is not born in the complete world. The source of all creations is the great Universe. This existence is the Creator and the source; namely, it is the sky before the sky that existed before everything came forth.

Let's imagine for a moment that we are this existence. From this existence where absolutely nothing exists, gas came forth and exploded into a fireball. The fireball cooled into solid matter, which became the stars in the sky. From the infinite Universe's point of view, the stars and the Universe are one; the star is the Universe and the Universe is the star. Everything that exists in the Universe is one with the Universe. If, like the Universe, one does not have false minds, then the individual is the whole and the whole is the individual. Everything is one; whether or not there is physical form, everything is oneness itself.

Everything that has been created is the Universe itself, the complete existence; thus, all things are without death. Even if the physical form disappears, the soul of that form is Truth. It is the eternal, never-dying immortal. That soul does not die because it is an individual entity that is one with the Universe that is Truth. The source of the Universe is Energy and God, and all forms are manifestations of this existence. The shape and form of this existence is everything in the world.

Man however, is not born in the world. He lives in his own mind: a shadow, a copy, of the real world. Hence, he is not complete and lives inside his illusionary mind. He is dead because his mind world is false and not real. Truth is the world and falseness is one's own mind that has taken pictures of the world. If one copies the world and lives inside what he has copied, he is not living in the world but in a picture - neither the world he lives in nor he himself living in that non-existent world exist.

The Human Soul

Whether or not man has a soul is something that is often discussed. The law of nature is that all material existences in the world come from the origin and go back to the origin. This is the law of the Universe. A person who believes in Truth, that is, a person who has become Truth, can be reborn in the kingdom of Truth. Only the master of Truth can enable him to be reborn, and can resurrect his soul.

The soul that man speaks of is false for it is an illusion that his false self mistakenly believes to exist in his own false mind. Therefore it is not really a soul. Those who say that man has a soul are those who have been born into a false world and they are those who speak as if they know things out of the ordinary. However, these people are dead because the world they think they have been born into is their own mind world.

Only a person who has the mind of Truth and is reborn in the kingdom of Truth has a soul that is alive; and only such a person has an everlasting soul. The human soul does not exist because man is a false image that does not exist in the world. However those who have souls will live, because they are reborn as the material of the origin that is the world.

It Is The Way Of The World That We Come From The Origin And Return Back To The Origin

There is no one in the world who knows the laws of the world or the will of the world. Religions often talk about heaven and hell, but the heaven and hell they speak of are false and delusional. When we become the great Universe itself - the master of the Universe - it is possible to know all the laws of the world.

Man and all creations in the world are the children of the origin, the source. It is the way of the world that we come from the origin and return to the origin. Don't all things in the world disappear eventually? Even when they disappear, the origin always just exists. If one is born from the origin, he is God and he is in the land of God. God is the existence that has been liberated from all things.

A person who talks about the ghost world, or hears voices, has a delusion born inside his mind. Only false things in a false world speak of knowing things out of the ordinary. God exists but does not dwell within his existence - his is the place free from all human conceptions and habits. It is the way of the world that man disappears after he dies. Only Truth, which has been resurrected in the world, becomes an eternal and never-dying immortal and can live forever in the land of God.

Hell is when one's self - a delusion in itself - lives inside his own delusions. These delusions do not exist, because they do not exist in the world. What exists in the world exists, and what does not exist in the world, does not exist. When it is said that Truth is everything just as one sees it, just as everything exists, it means that when man's mind becomes God - the mind of the world - what he sees that exists in the world actually exists. However if something does not exist in the world, it truly does not exist. In other words, the things that do not exist in the world are all human delusions.

The Relationship Between The Creator And Man

The original foundation is the Creator, and it is this existence that created the world and all things in it. It is not a material existence but a metaphysical one. It is a living existence that exists divinely as God and Soul. This existence created all material creations. It is omnipotent because all things in the world are the children, the creations, of this existence, and all things were created and given form by this existence. Simply put, it is omnipotent because it creates everything. All material things in the world were created by this existence; therefore they are its children and at the same time, they are this existence. This existence that is the origin and master created the material world, and all material things come from the origin and return to it. This is the way of the world.

However, there is a way for all material things to live forever. When man's mind becomes the world and the world is born with the body and mind of Truth, the origin, and the original foundation, the world will live forever in the land of Truth. This is something that cannot be done by man, no matter how hard he tries; it can only be done by the Creator - the master of the world - when this existence comes to the world as a human-being. At this time, the master of the world will take man to the world, so that he can be born and live there. This is the right, the authority, of the Creator.

In the Bible, it says that people cannot live unless they are reborn by the word of God and that only God can give salvation. This spiritual creation can only be done by the master of the true world; by the master of the world of Truth.

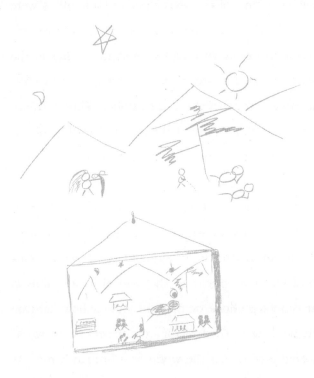

A Blessing From God Is Wisdom, Not Words

Many people say they received a blessing from God while praying in the mountains. Some claim to have heard God's voice which they believe to be a blessing, but they are mistaken. Whatever they heard came from their individual mind worlds because this is where people live. Anything they heard were just sounds from their mind worlds and not the voice of God.

Man is false and when he repents his sins, Truth enters him. He is enlightened and knows Truth to the extent of his absolution; namely, to the extent his unclean sins have disappeared. This is a true blessing from God. One whose body and mind has become one with the body and mind of God knows all the laws of the world because the consciousness of God has become him. His human wisdom changes to the wisdom of God, which is true knowing and blessing itself.

Only one who has been absolved of his sins can have the wisdom of God and only when the sinner dies and becomes reborn as the son of God can he live as a forever living and never-dying immortal. Man's sin is defying God and doing just as one pleases by possessing his own mind that is separate from God.

Only those who have repented their sins will become one with God, which will happen to the extent that their sins have been absolved. The place one goes to when the self dies is the sublime place of God. Without holding one's own living funeral, that is, without dying in the mind while living, any comments one makes about God are delusional sounds from within one's self; they are only the sounds of selfish desires. I heard many people who claimed to have heard the voice of God later say that nothing of significance was fulfilled despite what they heard. All they heard were the sounds of their desires, their selves.

Religion

In all the religions that have ever existed in this world, people listened to the words of past saints and they tried to adhere to those words from within their mind worlds. The saints all spoke of a complete being coming to the world one day and that at this time all men could become complete and live in a world where man is able to live forever without death. Essentially, they were all prophecies.

In Christianity it is said that a complete person will come to the world and take us to heaven and in Buddhism it is said that *Maitreya* will come to the world to save mankind. They indicate that this entity, the master of the heaven amongst heavens, will come to the world. Salvation is when this entity comes in human form to take people to the true heaven of the world in which they live, enabling them to live forever.

It is the way of the world that we live once, then die. Now consider for a moment that you had never been born in the world. Doesn't the world still exist? That world has existence when you exist, and if that world does not exist, only the original foundation, the emptiness that is the original shape and form of the Universe where nothing exists, remains. This existence is the Creator that is the origin and the source, and the heaven amongst heavens, which is Truth.

Only when this existence comes in human form can people be reborn as Truth, because this existence is Truth. Only this existence is the Savior. All religious scriptures are prophecies of being reborn as Truth and living forever in the land of Truth. Only this existence that is Truth is the complete person and only this being can give man salvation. Even though each religion waits for the coming of this existence, this existence of Truth does not exist in the mind of man because his mind lives inside an illusion. Thus man is unable to know when this existence has come, or gone. He is unable to know, because he only looks at outward appearances and has no Truth within his mind.

In Biblical times, the Jewish people were bound in their preconceptions to their interpretations of the Old Testament and were unable to recognize the existence of Jesus Christ when he came, and to this day they do not believe in Christ. Today's religious followers, each bound to their religious scriptures, are no different from the Jewish people of old who were unable to recognize the coming and going of the true Savior.

During the time of incompletion religions spoke of and handed down the words of saints. However, the time of completion will come, and man becoming complete in this time of completion is Truth.

Man is incomplete because he is false and fake; he lives in his own world made by taking pictures of the world, of the land of

Truth. He is dead and a sinner because he betrays the original master, the master of the world and the origin; he copies the master's world and makes it his own world. Emptying and discarding this mind world is repentance and penitence. If one has completely destroyed his world and his self also no longer exists, he is able to go to the world of the master. Being born and living in the heaven amongst heavens, which is the master, is the land of the true heaven. The place where this is accomplished is the place where the ultimate purpose of all religions is realized. Instead of being bound to one's wrongful preconceptions, he who comes to the place where one can actually become Truth and repents, will live.

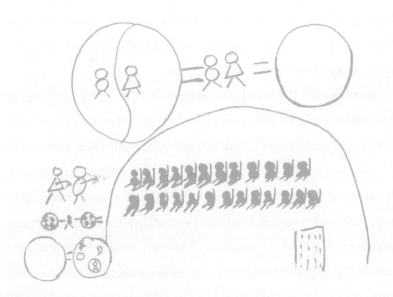

Why The Holy Writings Of Saints Cannot Be Heard Or Understood

The holy writings of saints are often read and even memorized, but no one understands their true meaning. This is because they were written from the perspective of Truth, the true world and unless one becomes this viewpoint, he inevitably reads them from his own perspective. Man is an entity that lives in his mind, his own world instead of the true world; thus he does not exist in the true world. True heaven does not exist in him, so he is unable to understand or hear the stories of the land of heaven. If he comes out from living within his self, his mind world, he becomes the true world and when he reads the holy writings from this perspective, there is nothing he cannot understand because he has become the holy writings.

Man lives his life wandering because he does not realize where he presently exists. He needs to realize that the place he is in is a video, a world of hell, and he must come out from that world of illusion by repenting. Countless religious denominations exist because each person's mind is different, and each person interprets the holy writings from the perspective of his human mind, ignorant of their true meaning. However, these interpretations are in the end just word-play and none of them can make man real.

The true way to know the meaning of the holy writings is to become the saints who wrote them. If one gets rid of the self-made picture world that has turned its back on the world, he will become a saint. Then, he will know everything.

The Importance Of Man

Whenever I meet people, I treat each and every person with serious consideration. I urgently implore them again and again to become Truth. Everyone seems to listen at the time, but many people suddenly change their minds and give up. Over the years that I have taught Truth, I learned that the human mind cannot be trusted. There is a Korean expression that describes how fickle it is: "While you can know what is in the depths of ten feet of water, the shallows of the human mind are unfathomable." Above all else, people need to realize that we only have one life, and if we do not accomplish Truth during our one lifetime in this age of becoming Truth, we may lose the chance to live eternally. Out of pity and concern, I urge people to cleanse their minds without giving up but people who live within their sins and karma ultimately end up following them. Isn't this the shape and form of their karma?

Man is unable to live like the flowing water, to live along with the passing years. He is unable to live mindlessly; that is, he cannot live without human minds. He is unable to become Truth because the greed with which he tries to achieve Truth himself, and his own will and purpose are far from Truth. One who tries to achieve Truth with his self is not able to do so, while one who knows that his self is an entity that must be discarded - he who knows that he is the worst person in the world - is able to accomplish everything and follow Truth. One whose false self thinks he is superior finds it difficult to achieve Truth because his superior self tries to possess Truth. A person who repents his sins knows Truth is more important than his self and it is precisely such a person who is able to meditate. Only he who has discarded his false self can be born as God, his real self. In this age of living and dying, let us all live by cleansing our sins and karma.

Man's Fate Is At A Crossroads Of Eternal Life And Death

There are often more days of difficulty and suffering than there are days of happiness in life and it is in the midst of difficult times that we begin to think about certain matters. I am sure there are many who have given some thought to where they will go after they die, though they will never find the answer within their human thoughts. This is because man's consciousness is dead and instead of living in the real world he is living inside the mind that he has made.

People seek out religion and other institutions in pursuit of Truth because they are incomplete. The ultimate goal of all of these institutions is to live forever. In other words, in their efforts to find a way to live eternally, people seek out religion, pursue Truth in various places and eventually come to places like Maum Meditation. However, the only way for people to live forever is to be reborn in the land of the Creator, the origin, and Truth.

One must live in an eternal place, namely, one must live in the land of Truth, in order to live forever. To get to this land, he must first destroy all of his falseness and then he must be reborn there; without doing this no one can live forever. In other words, only a person who completely discards his entire body and mind is able to go to the land of this existence, the land of Truth.

While on the cross, Jesus asked why God had forsaken him, but he was still willing to die if it was God's will. This means he was willing to discard himself and stand on the side of God who is Truth; he loved God and Truth more than he loved himself. It was through Jesus' death that the way was set to cross over into the land of God.

Everyone living in this world is a sinner. When the sinner completely dies, only Truth remains, and this world is heaven - it is the world of Truth and God. No one can live forever unless his self, the sinner, completely dies and he is reborn as a righteous person. Again, every single person in this world is a sinner. So the only way to live in heaven for eternity is to repent fully and be completely absolved of all sins. Then he will have the righteous world in his mind and he will be resurrected as a righteous person.

Unless one's mind becomes one with the righteous world and he is reborn in this world while he is still living, he will die forever. He who has completely destroyed his false self is one who has won the battle against his self. There is no way to live forever without eliminating the false sinner within and being born as a righteous person, as Truth.

God, Buddha And Heaven Are Within Man's Mind

If you ask what Buddha is, Buddhism tells us that you are Buddha and that your mind is Buddha. Although this is correct, only a person who has the mind of Buddha is Buddha. Buddha, God, and heaven, do not exist in the human mind.

The human mind is the mind of one's own world, made by copying the real world. When one lives in such a world which has turned against the real world, that world is false, non-existent and illusionary. Although man may think that he is alive, he is dead because he lives in this illusionary world - a world that is not alive.

In other words, the world is real but the mind world of pictures taken of the world is false. Man is an entity that lives inside a "videotape" that he has made. This is why man is incomplete, and in order to become complete, he takes up a religion, cleanses his mind and seeks Truth. Even now, many people all over the world are striving to achieve human completion.

Man does not exist in the real world because he lives inside this picture world; he does not have life and is therefore dead. God, Buddha and heaven do not exist inside such a mind - the human mind. When this mind is discarded and one returns to the mind of the true world, the mind of the origin, what is real and true - Buddha, God, heaven - will be within him, within his mind. Only he who has God and Buddha within him can know God and Buddha; only he who has heaven within can know heaven.

This existence that is Truth, the origin, is the master of the world that created the world. When this true existence becomes one's mind, God, Buddha and heaven will be within him.

He who has become this mind has the mind of the world; he has the whole world within him. Therefore heaven is right where he is, and God that is Buddha is within him; the world becomes his mind. On the other hand, he who has the false picture world inside his mind is in a world of hell. Not only is he living in hell now, it is where he stays even after death because this world is the only one that exists within him. Simply put, a person in the picture world goes to hell while a person who has the mind of the original foundation, of Truth, will live forever in the land of Truth.

It Is The Age When All Wars Cease To Exist, And All People Become Of One Mind By Self-Reflection And Repentance

From an age when the world was moved by the human mind, it is changing to an age of the world becoming man's mind. Namely, the age of nature's flow has begun. When man becomes the mind of the world by casting off his self-centered and narrow mind, he will become broad-minded, or "big" minded, and have no human minds. Therefore, his mind will always be at leisure. Narrow minds filled with greed and attitudes that only one's self is right and other people are wrong have given rise to countless wars everywhere; innumerable people have died from wars because of the incomplete human mind. When man's mind becomes the mind of the world, everyone will become one. People will accept and understand each other; and because there will no longer be any narrow-minded greed, all wars will cease to exist.

What Is Truth; What Is The Existence Of Truth?

Worldly preconceptions teach us that Truth is something that is eternal and never-changing. I, too, teach that Truth is eternal, never-changing and living. I also teach what worldly preconceptions do not - what the existence of Truth is. It is the place before all material form was created; in other words, Truth is the emptiness that remains when you take away everything in the sky that is the Universe - the stars, the sun, the moon and the Earth and even all material substances from the air.

Truth, the emptiness, is an existence that is alive; it existed before the beginning, exists now and will continue to exist for all eternity. This existence is the origin of Truth. Everything that exists in the world appeared from this place of non-existence. Since all creation came from this existence, whether or not those creations exist, they are this existence.

This existence always just exists, but man cannot see or know this existence that is the origin and the source because it does not exist in his mind. The human mind is a mind that takes pictures of the world. The sky or the Universe inside a picture is not alive, which is why man is not able to know this existence. It is not possible to see or know this existence unless one's mind becomes one with it.

This existence is the living God which existed before the beginning of time and which will continue to exist after the whole world has disappeared. Religions call this existence God, Buddha, Allah and the Creator, amongst other things. This existence is the master of the world that created the whole of the Universe. All material forms in this world come from and go back to this existence; this is Truth and the way of the world. Where do all the numerous people, animals and plants go after living on the Earth? Haven't they vanished? Haven't all these things gone back to the place of non-existence, the emptiness, which is the origin and the source of everything? This is the way of the world. Whether or not something exists in material form, it is always this existence.

When the existence of Truth comes to this world in human form, the world can be reborn as the body and mind of this existence in the world of this existence, namely, heaven. Then this world of heaven is the eternally living land with no death. This world is a spiritual land beyond material existence. It is the land of the Holy Father and the Holy Spirit, the land of *Dharmakaya* and *Sambhogakaya* and the land of the Soul and Spirit.

Heaven is the place where the material realm in this world has been reborn in the land of the origin as the Soul and Spirit of the origin. Nothing that is material in the world is eternal; however, the sky of the Universe - the existence of Truth - is eternal. Therefore, only when one is reborn with the body and mind, the

Jung and *Shin* of the original sky, which is the heaven amongst heavens, can he become Truth and live for eternity. Truth is that which exists; it is eternal, never-changing and alive. The empty sky, where all material things have been eliminated, is the source, the essence and the original Truth.

Idealism

Idealism is Truth itself: the state of completeness. To be ideal is to become Truth; it is when all of one's thoughts and actions are oriented towards Truth. Therefore, an ideal life is when one is born as Truth and lives as Truth.

The reason idealism has not been realized in religion, even though they aim towards it, is they do not have the method to get to the state of idealism. Therefore, they only talk of what is ideal through scriptures, and are unable to reach the ideal world. There are tens of thousands of different religious sects because the scriptures have been interpreted by those who have not gone to the ideal world and human thoughts have become the scriptures. True idealism is reaching the ideal world, and being reborn in the ideal world itself. Then, such a world will be realized.

The way to realize this is to ignore and eliminate one's false self. The origin exists when the false self is gone. When he is then reborn in the mind of the origin, this is the ideal world.

Imagine for a moment that you had never been born - the world still exists. Even if the stars, the moon, the Earth and everything on Earth had not been born, the empty sky that is the emptiness still exists. This is the origin, the source, God and the

Creator. When one returns to the mind of this existence itself, and is reborn here as the substance of the empty sky, this place is heaven; it is the ideal world.

Idealism is the thoughts, actions, and life of a person who has gone to this world.

When the realization of idealism becomes possible, it will become an ideal world.

The true ideal world is when the world becomes one mind, when without separation between you and me, the world lives as one.

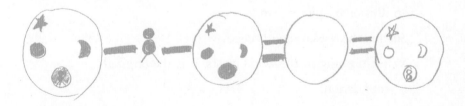

Salvation Comes To Pass Only When The Master Of The Original Foundation Comes As A Human-being

The world is enlightened,

but man living in the false world, is not enlightened.

All creations come from the original foundation,

live in the original foundation,

and return to it.

But having lost the original foundation,

man has a world of his own mind with which he lives,

and the original foundation does not exist in his mind.

Originally, man's mind and the world are one

but man has taken pictures of the world inside his mind,

and he lives in this world of his mind;

an illusionary picture world.

Such is the reason man is dead.

When nothing in the world exists, it is the original

　　foundation,

and when everything exists, it is still the original foundation.

Those who become the mind of the original foundation

will always live in the original foundation.

But those in their mind worlds live inside that world always, and when they die,

they will die forever since they do not have life.

Currently, the average life span for men is around seventy-six years, and for women it is eighty-one years. People are not born in the world only to die and disappear after living to the end of their life span. The purpose, the reason, people live is to live eternally in the completed land without death. In order for a person to live in this land, he must realize that he and his own world are false, destroy this false world, and be reborn as the substance of Truth in the land of Truth. Only then can he live forever. If, while one is living, his mind returns to the original foundation, the true existence, and he is reborn with the body and mind of this existence, he regains his original body and mind - he comes to his true senses. Such a person will live forever even after his body dies because he has been born again and resurrected within the land of his mind while he is still living.

Let's assume for a moment, that you have been burned to death. Even so, your self that has been born as Truth would still exist. One who does not have the original foundation that is life and resurrection within him, does not have life and therefore he is dead. When he dies, he is dead and disappears. If he repeatedly and completely eliminates his false body and mind, the original foundation - God - will live.

It is the way of the world that everything in the world comes from the original foundation, lives in the original foundation, and returns to the original foundation. Only when the master - the true owner - of the original foundation comes as a human-being, can the whole world be saved in the land of the original foundation.

The Time Of Subtraction When Man Can Fulfill Human Completion Has Begun

Man is born with a mind that wants to possess, so he seeks satisfaction and happiness through possession. However, there is no end to such means; ultimately, he cannot be satisfied or happy.

All greed arises from his mind of inferiority and when he is not able to have or achieve what he wants, this turns into feelings of regret and bitterness. Only when he discards his greed, will those feelings of regret and bitterness truly disappear.

Until now, man has lived trying to possess what he can because of his mind that wants to make everything his. At present, this is the way all people live.

The world is in a state of instability; people have lost their trust in each other and they live struggling to appease their feelings of inferiority. Rather than learning how to possess more, in this age learning how not to possess is the way to become complete and live a better life. This is because instead of just thinking that we must discard money in our minds, we will be able to carry it out into action.

A mind full of greed is always anguished; and a life lived following one's anguish is without action; it is a life with thoughts leading only to more thoughts.

If the past was the age of adding to one's mind, now is the age of subtracting what is in his mind. A person who subtracts his minds in this time will recover his original nature. Consequently, the whole human race will become one and the world will become complete because everyone will live for others and the world.

Human completion is becoming God's mind by subtracting all of one's own minds. One will then be able to live well for he will have wisdom and his mind that is the Soul and Spirit will live eternally.

Subtracting all human mind - all the mind one has, that he has "eaten" - is completion.

Part 2

The Human Mind

The human mind is an illusion, so it does not exist even though it may seem to exist. However, the mind of God - the mind of the world - is the entity of Truth which actually exists although it has no form.

Is The Mind Non-existence?

Some people say that the mind is non-existence. Non-existence means it does not exist. The human mind is an illusion, so it does not exist even though it may seem to exist. However, the mind of God - the mind of the world - is the entity of Truth which actually exists although it has no form. The true mind is the pure emptiness that remains after all material is subtracted from the Universe. This pure empty Universe, the sky, exists. Doesn't the sky still exist even after you are gone and the world is gone?

Some people say this existence, does not exist because it is non-material. However this existence is most certainly alive and its Soul and Spirit exist as oneness. Man and all the creations in the world are the representations of this existence. If asked what this existence looks like, the answer would simply be that everything in the world is this existence of Truth.

Because this existence is alive, it is the omnipotent Creator that creates everything in the whole world. When our minds become one with this existence, our minds are one with the mind of the world. Thus, one who is reborn in this world is without death.

For one who becomes the world, the world is his mind. Man's

mind does not exist because it is false. The mind of the Universe that is God is not nothingness; it is existence - a non-material real existence.

Man Has A Mind Of Hunger Which He Tries To Satiate By Devouring Whatever He Can

Man's mind holds illusions, which in themselves are hungry and empty minds. He always feels empty and hungry because he lives with these minds. The mind of hunger is a false mind that takes pictures. The human mind stores everything that it has stolen from the world; it is a mind that lives having turned away from Truth. Therefore man is a sinner and he is bound to his karma.

A characteristic of the human mind is to "eat" whatever it can, to have as much as it can, because only then can it boast of its own greatness and show off its false self. Man, for whom this characteristic has become a habit, keeps "eating" everything, but this only results in more burdens and suffering and he ends up dying inside this tomb. The human mind was created to re-semble the Universe that is God, but since it is not the mind of God itself, it devours everything in the Universe. However what it consumes is false and not true. Falseness is that which does not exist; it is one's own delusions and thoughts. The word "hunger" usually describes hunger for food. However, real hunger is the hunger of the mind - when our minds are filled with a void from falseness. This is the reason man is always hungry.

Until now man was not righteous and there was no method to stop one's mind from habitually consuming everything. This is the reason we have been living in a world of continuous wars where people live only for their own survival; a world without love where people hate each other. It has been a world with divisions between nations; where everything is clearly divided into what is yours and what is mine. It was this way because we made and protected our own mind worlds and adhered to our preconceptions and habits, unaware that we were doing so.

Man acts and speaks according to what he has devoured and stored in his mind. A person with a righteous mind will live righteously in the land of righteousness. Righteousness is eliminating all minds that one has devoured. Then it is possible to get to Truth and live righteously.

All People In The World Are Liars

People generally believe that they are truthful, honest and right. They commonly also think that they do not cheat anyone, and that they do good deeds for others. People have self-centered human minds which make them believe anything that is not theirs is wrong.

However, there is nothing right in people. That is, one's own preconceptions and habits are all wrong. From the viewpoint of Truth, the world, all of it is wrong because man lives in a false picture world that is a copy of the source, the origin. None of man's preconceptions and habits are right because all that is human is false. Everything he says is false because he can only talk about the pictures in him. All of his actions are also false.

There are those who claim to live not for themselves but for others, but when I tell them that even their good deeds were done essentially for themselves, they usually cannot help but agree. Since man lives in a shadow of the world and that shadow is within him, he can only speak of shadows. Therefore everything he says is a lie. A righteous person's words and actions are all true because he lives in the world and not in a shadow. Only a righteous person does not lie or act falsely. He speaks true words and does true deeds.

We Are Not Living In The Right Way

The reason the lives we humans live are false is the empty Universe - the original Truth and the original foundation - is our origin. That is to say, even if you had not been born, the emptiness that existed before all creation exists just as it is. You came into the human world with what you call your "self", and lived as that false self having made your own world inside your mind. From the perspective of the original foundation, your life is less than a second when compared to the eternal land of the original foundation; it is nothing more than eighty or so odd years.

Everyone lives according to his own will inside an illusionary world that he has made, turning his back on the original foundation, his true self. He does not know that the world he is living in is a dream, wherein he has his spouse and children, money, fame, family and love. Believing that the dream is his, he lives only for his own sake, amassing fortune in his world. How foolish this is! Furthermore, he leaves his fortune to his children; in effect, adding burden to their illusionary world. He is truly very foolish. He does not understand that possessing something - making something his - is suffering and burden. Therefore, he constantly tries to gain everything he can and fulfill his purpose. Within that burden and suffering, he dies eternally; which is why his illusionary world is meaningless.

What one truly needs to do and achieve is to completely destroy his false self, become true and live forever. How can a person be called righteous if he does not amass blessings in the land of Truth? One who lives for the sake of righteousness discards his self, and transfers his family, money, love and fame to the land of righteousness. Such a person is truly righteous; he is an eternal and never-dying immortal.

Man is certain that he is living in the world, but he is a false and incomplete being who lives inside his own mind that is an illusion. In other words, he is a ghost: a dream-like, non-existent being. He does not know the will of the true world and he only has selfish minds, so he lives by his own will inside his own world that he has made wherein he sees, hears, and learns. Believing that only he is right and everybody else is wrong, he lives only for his own sake with discontent and hunger endlessly trying to fill that void with his desires. However, this only results in suffering.

A ghost is an entity that dies and disappears, and as such, the only thing it is able to teach its children or other people is how to have its own particular brand of greed. We must teach our children of death before we teach them of life; we must teach them of not having before we teach them to possess; of non-existence before existence; and of Truth before falseness. We must teach our families as well as the people in this world to live for righteousness and to live in righteousness together. Living in such a way is a true and righteous life.

Do not become a pitiful person - the sort who thinks only of leaving money to your children and family, thus allowing them to die within their minds. It is only when you commit yourself to a true, righteous life while you are alive that the blessings from your life's actions will remain in the true world. A person who does not amass blessings in heaven while living cannot ultimately be born in the kingdom of heaven. This is because God within him is dead and he is more attached to his self that is a ghost.

The Meaning Behind "Words Becoming Seeds"

In Korea people believe that when they speak badly of someone or curse them, the words become reality and what is said actually happens - that the words become the "seed" of what happens in reality.

The true meaning behind this saying is that when the master of the true world comes, man will live if he tells him to live and die if he tells him to die. The words of the master of the world are life itself, so they become the "seeds" of life. They are seeds because his words create consciousness that is life. Furthermore, his words are seeds and life because they save people and allow the world to live.

The Bible tells us that God created the world with his words. It also says that no one can live unless they are reborn through his words. God is the master of the land of Truth, and his words are life itself. Only God can speak words of life. His words become the seeds of life, which means they create the world of Truth. This is solely the power of God. The expression "words will become seeds" means the same as "God will create the world and man through his words".

God's Mind Beyond Human Mind

Handsome, good-looking, stylish,

great figure, well groomed,

so good-looking, so distinguished,

so pretty, so lovely,

radiant as the moon, well-defined features,

he's a handsome man, she's a beautiful woman,

ugly, not good-looking, not stylish,

not glowing, weak features,

he's an ugly man; she's an ugly woman,

like, love,

clean, beautiful,

splendid, pretty,

do not like, do not love,

dirty, ugly,

not splendid, not pretty,

dead, alive,

it is this; it is that;

even the mind that the world exists is a human mind -

the mind of a ghost.

A ghost does not have the true mind

so it only sees outward appearances,

but God sees into the inner heart.

God's mind exists beyond the countless human minds.

God's mind knows nothing;

there is no feeling, no taste or smell,

there is nothing it sees or hears;

it is the mind where everything has ceased.

Even though God's mind is alive,

it does not dwell in its existence,

and while it is a mind of non-existence

where all have ceased,

it is a mind that is truly alive,

the mind of wisdom itself.

We have often heard that minds do not exist. This means the incalculable number of delusions piled up in the human mind do not exist. It is also said that the true mind does not exist; this is to say that the true mind does not have shape or form. It is not material, but it exists as *Jung* and *Shin*, the Soul and Spirit, which is Truth. This existence is the empty sky which remains when you take away every material thing in the sky.

This empty sky is the true mind. It is the origin, the source, the original foundation, and it is an entity that is alive. The world of this existence is heaven: a place where the world and people are born as the Soul and Spirit of this existence.

The human mind is pictures and an illusion; God's mind is reality - what truly exists. God's mind is the true mind; the mind of the empty sky. The human mind is the false mind that has taken pictures of all that belongs to the world. Man lives inside that false mind so if he discards all the pictures, his mind will be changed from the human mind to God's mind.

The Human Mind I

Man's eyes, nose, ears, mouth and body were made as picture-taking tools from birth, and his mind is where the pictures taken of the world are stored. What we call sin or karma is taking pictures of that which belongs to the world and living in those pictures in one's mind, instead of having a mind that is one with the world. Such a person is a sinner - one who has accumulated karma - because he has betrayed the origin that is the world by making and living in his own world.

When man dies after living in the world, he ends up dying forever because he lives in an illusion, a world that does not exist in the real world. However one who has been absolved of all his sins and has been reborn in Truth is an eternal immortal. Man does not know this because his mind is overlapping the world and he mistakenly thinks he is living in the real world. His sin is living in an illusionary world that he himself has made in his own mind. This is why life is futile; why life is that of a weed, a cloud, a bubble and something that does not, simply does not, exist.

Man, whose mind is false, is always hungry, which is why he constantly tries to consume things, and tries to gain and seek Truth from what he has consumed. However, such actions only add more falseness to falseness; adding ever more suffering and burden. Only by discarding those burdens, and by this path only, can one truly become Truth.

While the time of incompletion was the period of addition and gain, the time of completion is one of subtraction. If one eliminates all that is false, only what is true will remain. Because man is false he can become true when he is eliminated. Those who try to gain Truth while holding onto falseness cannot achieve Truth, and even if they do achieve it, it is false.

The human mind is one's own world that he made by taking pictures of the world and engraving his emotions therein; emotions made by what he has seen, heard, smelled and felt in his mind. The human mind only has pictures; it is an illusionary mind that is self-centered and selfish - a mind that knows only itself.

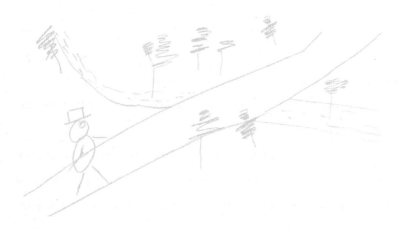

Man Ends Up Following His Mind - If There Is Falseness In His Mind He Will Follow Falseness, If He Seeks Truth He Will Follow Truth

In the world, there is no such thing as a free lunch. That is, one acquires as much wealth and material things as the effort he has put into acquiring them. For example, in Maum Meditation, some people were not able to finish the levels due to their karma. They could only reach a certain level of meditation because of the size of their minds, and the karma they had accrued. That is to say, their minds did not have the capacity to take in more.

I have met many narrow-minded people who were not thankful at all to people who taught them something; they believe that what they learned was accomplished on their own because of some superior quality of theirs. Because their minds did not have the capacity to fully take in what they had learned, they later spoke of what was in their minds - what they said was only their own preconceptions.

Even though many people live in this world, no two people are of the same mind. This is because everyone has his own mind. The mind one has is false so no matter how much Truth is spoken to him, he cannot understand or hear it because he does not have Truth within him. Jesus said that people cannot see although they have eyes to see and they cannot hear although they have ears to hear. This means that man is shackled to his mind and he does not know anything that is not within him. However what is in him is all false; it is not true.

When man's false mind becomes the mind of the world which is true, man will be able to understand the laws of the world. Only then will he see the world as it is and only then will he know Truth. Knowing Truth is only possible when one's mind becomes Truth.

Man only sees the outer form, but Truth sees whether the mind within is true. Man keeps scraps in his mind - everything he has learned and all that has happened to him - but these things are far from Truth, and they cause him to lose his human nature and care only about himself. If man recovers his human nature, the world will become truly peaceful. It will become a world where people can trust and believe in one another.

When one's preconceptions and habits are thrown away, he will be able to accept everything in the world. The world will become a good place to live, as people's narrow, negative minds become positive, practical and active. Life unfolds according to what is in one's mind, and this is the same even in the false human world. If one has lived for money and academic achievements, these things will exist in his mind and his life in the future will re-volve around these things.

Academics, the law and all that is man-made in the world will naturally disappear with time. The world where people live without the mind of self - in other words, the world of saints or righteous people - will be a truly joyful place to live, for all people will be of one mind. Without the minds of suffering and burden, there will be days of endless laughter. It will be a world without division between nations; a just world where people are honored to live for others; a world where people work with laughter and live joyfully; a world where all people live well. There will be no fear of death because people will live forever with heaven existing within them, and their selves born in heaven. This world and the world beyond will become one.

Man Does Not Know When The Savior Has Come Or Gone

Man's mind is false. He does not know Truth because he does not have Truth in him. The world that he lives in is the world of his mind. He has never been born in the world that is true, which is why he does not know Truth. There has never been a true person in the world because man is a sinner who takes pictures of what belongs to the world. He has these pictures in his mind so he thinks that they and the world are one and the same. In other words, he is under the delusion that he is really living in the world because the world of his mind and the real world overlap. This is why man does not know the true world that is the land of God.

The Savior is the origin, the Creator and Truth. Man is waiting for the Savior to come because only when this existence comes as a human-being, can man and all of creation be reborn in the land of Truth. However when this Savior does come, man will only see his outward appearance and will not be able to recognize his mind - the mind of the origin. Hence, he will not know even when the existence of the Savior has come. This existence will enable falseness to become Truth; he will enable man to be reborn and resurrected in the true land. Aren't we looking to religion and searching for the way to Truth because people are incomplete? If there is a place where one becomes complete and falseness becomes real, then isn't this the place where the Savior can be found?

The Savior is the master of the land of Truth that is the origin. This existence that comes as a human-being and saves man and the world in the land of Truth is the Savior. This existence is the living God. Material creation was done by Truth that is the origin, and when Truth comes in human form, as a person, it is a person that will enable all existence in the Universe to live in the land of Truth and the origin. This is the completion of the Universe. The Savior is beyond the human mind of preconceptions and habits; the Savior is of the mind, beyond physical form, so only a person who has this existence in his mind will know the Savior.

A person who repents his sins and karma in order to become this existence will know the Savior. The easiest way for man to find the Savior is to find the place where he can be absolved of his sins and karma; the place where he can become real and complete. Then, he will also be able to find the Savior.

A Sense Of Inferiority

Human desires differ from person to person but every desire is manifested from feelings of inferiority: of feeling not good enough or having less than other people. A person who lacks love seeks love and a person who lacks money chases money. The powerless seek power and he who has had his pride trampled on seeks to regain his pride. What one felt he lacked during his developmental years becomes his sense of inferiority. For example, if a woman suffers abuse from her mother-in-law, she will in turn be harsh to her daughter-in-law because she has that mind. One pursues what he desires and these arise from the innumerable minds that he has; they are all expressions of his mind.

There is a saying that things happen according to the mind one has. This means that one lives exactly according to the mind that he has taken in - no more and no less. What one eats is excreted through urine and feces but man has never excreted any of the countless minds he has consumed from birth and he lives with the burdens, suffering, worries and anxieties that they bring.

Those minds are all pictures taken of what belongs to the world, and he is dead in the world of that mind, which itself is a picture. He strives to achieve within that picture world but his actions and deeds are all false because he lives according to the script of that mind.

The world beyond the world, that is, the world beyond the human mind that has been eliminated, is the true land; a real world that is not a picture. When this real world is inside one's mind, his feelings of inferiority will disappear and he will have only the highest mind of Truth. He who is born in this place is God; he is one who has shed all human minds and he is one who is free. It is because of the pictures in one's mind that there are conflicts and obstacles while living in the world. When this fixed framework of mind is gone, those conflicts and obstacles also disappear and he will be able to live better than he did before.

Acceptance is the absence of judgment and discrimination; when one sees things just as they are, when he just lives. If one has a framework of pictures in his mind, then many things catch in his mind and bother him, which cause him to blame others and the world. No one in the world blames himself instead of other people. But because your mind exists, everything is your fault. When the people of the world can blame themselves, everyone will have an accepting mind; they will be able to live without conflict and everyone will live well. When man eliminates the false world that he has eaten, he will live a life of nature's flow and he will be able to live well because he will no longer have feelings of inferiority.

When people act with minds that originate from feelings of

inferiority, they will act as the worst evil. These actions will only bring more evil as their result; evil begets evil. However the evil will end up dying within evil. Within evil, the evil will live with pain and heavy burdens.

One Who Tries To Become Enlightened While Holding Onto His Self Will Fail, While One Who Knows That His Self Is A False Wrongful Entity And Truly Discards Himself Will Be Enlightened And Become Truth To The Extent That He Has Discarded

Many people seek out Maum Meditation because they want to find a way to assuage their feelings of inferiority. There are also many who have wandered from place to place, trying to find a way to fulfill their desires and resolve their regrets and bitterness. However, one thing that is certain is that all those who have tried to find or fulfill something with their selves were only able to meditate to the point where they met their limitations, after which they departed.

Man takes pictures in his mind of everything in the originally existing world, and lives making everything his. However, these things are all false and become his sins and karma. Man lives in this falseness. Therefore a person who discards everything in his world that he has seen, heard, felt and what he feels is his, and he who knows his self is false and therefore discards his sins and karma, can accomplish Truth.

There are only a few people in the world who attain what they pursue and desire. Those who fail to obtain their desires commonly blame the circumstances of their life, but this then gives them a chance to reflect back on their life. Many, realizing their wretchedness, come to Maum Meditation to seek and achieve something in order to better their circumstances but this mind only exists in their minds; the minds they have do not exist in the minds of other people.

Human sin is the sin of having betrayed the world, so a person who knows that he is a sinner and denies his self can accomplish Truth. However a person who meditates holding onto himself is still false even if he accomplishes Truth. One's false self is his own worst enemy, for it is the worst and most foolish entity in the world. He mistakenly thinks he is alive but he is actually living in an illusionary picture world - a world that does not exist and is made by stealing what belongs to the true world. He can only accomplish completion if he relentlessly denies this false self.

The world is complete but man lives inside his mind of illusions and pictures. In order to throw away his own world and enter the real world, he must completely deny himself. This is the study of Maum Meditation - denying one's self completely and becoming one with the mind of the world that is Truth by discarding all of his preconceptions, habits and mind world.

One who denies his self, and does not try to achieve with his false self, is able to do the meditation more easily. He can accomplish human completion while he is living, and can live forever in heaven, the kingdom of Truth. His Soul and Spirit will live there without death. Those who do not have the true Soul and Spirit, Truth, will die forever when their bodies pass away. However, for a person who has the mind of the world, the kingdom of Truth, within him, his Soul and Spirit will be reborn in that kingdom and he will live there forever.

One Speaks And Acts According To What His Mind Holds

The mind world of man, filled with what belongs to the world, is not real but false images. One who is inside those false images can only speak of what his mind holds but these are only his preconceptions and opinions. Since those who live in the false human world can only speak and act according to what is in their minds, those who speak and act in a way that fits the time they are in live a slightly better life. Their lives and actions reflect the minds that they have taken in.

In any case, the human mind has made a selfish self-made world that cares only about himself. In this world, doing well for himself, being the best and boasting about himself is everything.

However when his human mind disappears and becomes God's mind, man will live a truly joyful life. He will live divinely; he will have complete freedom and liberation, be without worries and work in the land of God. Being selfless - literally having no self - he will work for the benefit of others and live amassing blessings in the land of righteousness while he is alive. Since the land of righteousness has no death, he will know the oneness of life and death. The land of forever-living immortals where one does not die after death but lives as God, is the land of righteousness. This is what it means for what is false to become true.

When man becomes a true person and he lives as one, he will also do well in society, in the world. The best path for all people is to become complete and true because the correct definition of living well is to live as Truth and live in the land of righteousness.

The first priority in education should be to teach people to become Truth before teaching them the skills and knowledge to make a living. If this happens, the entire world will become more prosperous. This is because people will live for others if the level of their consciousness become higher, or in other words if they come to their original senses. Only when we change our minds to that of Truth that is God, will we be able to live together as one.

When we are reborn with the mind of the sky - or in Korean, *Haneol*, which literally means one mind - everyone will have wisdom; no one will behave foolishly, and we will no longer be trapped in our individual mind worlds. Our actions will produce true results and everyone will live well and happily. Changing our minds from the false mind to the true mind is the most urgent matter at hand. When this happens, it will become a world where people can live with ease of mind.

Those Who Follow *Dō*

The reasons people follow or do *dō* (a Korean word meaning Truth or The Way) is in order to succeed, to become superior to other people in some way, or to appease their feelings of inferiority. However, *dō* is the opposite of these things because the existence of *dō* is the existence of Truth. In order to achieve true *dō*, one must discard his very self and shed all of his own preconceptions and habits. Only then is it possible to get to the place of *dō*. However many people fail because they try to achieve *dō* whilst holding onto their selves.

Dō is falseness becoming real. One's false self needs only to be discarded but if one tries to gain *dō* within himself he ultimately fails because *dō* cannot be contained within something that is false. The "evil spirits" or "demons" spoken of in the Bible refer to one's false self.

In Buddhism, achieving *dō* is spoken of as being more difficult than scratching one's way out of a silver-iron mountain. It is a metaphor highlighting how strongly man has made his own mind world and how difficult it is to detach his false self.

When one completely discards his self, then in fact he achieves what he originally desired - he becomes a truly superior person and triumphs over his feelings of inferiority. However he who seeks to gain something in his own world is ultimately unable to gain what he seeks and only adds to his karma. It is important to know the principle that nothing can be gained for free in the world - such is the way of the world. There are many who try to achieve Truth without putting in the effort. They are showing the habit with which they have always lived. Man behaves and lives in the way dictated by the form of his mind. Thus, it can be said that man shows the "price" of his form. Whether or not one is able to achieve Truth also shows the price of his mind's form. One's form always pays its price.

The Misconceptions About *Dŏ*

Images that arise in the mind are all illusions. Furthermore, everything that one sees and hears is an illusion also, because they are seen and heard from within his mind. Many people want to do *dŏ* - pursue Truth - in order to become superior or to gain something. However *dŏ* is about discarding; simply put, it is about discarding all of one's mind and body so that nothing remains. This is so that his mind can become the never-changing existence of Truth, from which he can then be reborn.

Only when the master of *dŏ* comes to the world, will there be a method to achieve *dŏ*. Such a method had not existed in the world thus far because the true existence of *dŏ* had not yet come to the world. People frequently talk about *Maitreya*, the Savior, *Jung-do-ryung*, or the Great Leader who will come to the world. All of these expressions and prophecies mean that the master of the world - the master of *dŏ* - will come.

People are living inside their minds, that is, they have turned against *dŏ*. Therefore, *dŏ* is discarding man's body and mind that has turned against *dŏ*. It can also be explained by saying that it is falseness going towards Truth, and that it is falseness becoming real. It can further be said that *dŏ* is man's mind becoming the true consciousness - the mind of the original foundation. To "achieve" *dō* is to come out into the true world from the illusionary world. It is harder for man who is false to achieve *dō* than it is for him to claw his way out from within an iron mountain. There is a Korean saying that it is harder to triumph over one's self than it is to win a war against a million soldiers. This saying must surely refer to achieving *dō*.

While teaching *dō*, I have found that people try to achieve it while holding onto their selves. Their false selves want to have Truth, so in the end, they are still false. The stronger one's sense of inferiority is, the more he wants to gain something by doing *dō*. I have often found that such people eventually become possessed. This happens because they try to achieve *dō* without discarding themselves. There are also cases of people who are still in their mind worlds, deluding themselves that they are in the heaven of Truth, and they claim to be born in heaven. There are still others who claim that they have come from heaven. These are all cases of people who were reborn in their mind worlds. Although they must get to the original foundation by discarding, they drift further away from this path and only add to their sins. This usually happens to those who have many sins. It happens because of their greed; and what one sees and knows from this world is seen and known by ghosts that are delusions.

When one becomes the mind of the original foundation in the original foundation, one comes to know Truth through wisdom. When one claims he sees, hears or knows something out of the ordinary, they are just voices from within himself, the ghost. This is called megalomania in modern psychiatry. When other people get caught in someone else's megalomania, they also become patients of a joint or collective megalomania. In certain areas of world, rites are performed that invoke a spirit to enter a person who is a spiritual medium. This kind of thing is no different from cases of joint megalomania. When one claims to be able to see another world in heaven and speaks of things that are out of the ordinary, it is an effort to fulfill his greed and it is an expression of his sense of inferiority.

When people who are on the same "wavelength" as he is become caught in his demented mind - his false mind world - they speak and behave in the same way as he does, without knowing that they are also demented. Together they are in a world of shared collective megalomania, and their actions are those of ghosts who are unable to wake from a dream. Ghosts and collective ghosts are delusions.

A soul that is born into existence in the world of Truth is liberated from death, birth, aging and sickness. He is in the place of freedom; beyond desires, anger, foolishness, the five desires and seven sins. It is the place where all knowing has ceased. Sometimes, a person gets a glimpse of this world and puts an image of it inside his mind, claiming that he has received a crown or that he is the master of this world. Such a person is speaking from within his mind world. His actions are those of a ghost, a delusion, which happens because he is unable to discard himself; they are a manifestation of his sense of inferiority giving rise to a mind of greed.

God and heaven only exist in one's mind which has become one with the world. Only then does the world that is the land of God and the original foundation exist in his mind. This world does not exist in one's mind of delusion. Images that exist and arise in one's mind are not the world of God, but his own false mind world. Such a person ends up dying for eternity. There is the old adage, "birds of a feather flock together". In the same way, people suffer from a shared, collective megalomania because they are similar people who have "flocked together". In any case, whenever somebody says that he has had a divine revelation or that he has heard something supernatural, it is all coming from within his illusionary mind world.

All People End Up Dying - Everyone Who Does Not Become Truth While Living Will End Up Dying

Many people wonder about what happens after death, but man does not have the answer or solution to this question. While all people of every religion believe that they will go to heaven, they end up dying because they live inside the mind worlds that they themselves have made.

This is because the human mind world is a picture world copied from the real world; a world where one lives having put what is the world's inside him. A person living in his mind does not exist because he is false. Just as one's self that was recorded and seen on a videotape is an image and not real, man is dead because he is not born in the world and he does not have the Soul and Spirit of Truth. He is dead because his soul has not been resurrected. In the mind world that the false self, the delusion, has drawn or made, its attachments lead him to believe that the false self - the shadow of the fleshly human body - is what lives.

People also eat and talk in a video, but what happens in the video is not real. Only what is born in the world is real; man is false because he lives inside a video that has recorded the world. A person who is alive has the mind of the world but a person whose true soul is not born inside his mind ends up dying forever because he does not have a true soul.

Changing the human mind of pictures to God's mind is repentance and true penitence. Man is not real - he has not born in the real land - so when he dies, he ends up dying forever. A person who has become real remains alive because his Soul and Spirit has been born. Those who completely discard their false selves, go to the real land and are reborn in that land, are the only ones who will live. Everybody else will die.

Only When You Die Can You Know The World Beyond

When a person in Korea does not have the solution to a dilemma he will often be told, "You will know the world beyond (the afterworld) only after you die." However no one in this world knows with certainty about the world beyond. In religion it is often said that those who do good deeds will go to heaven and those who do evil deeds will go to hell. Yet there is no clear answer to this question: Does the world beyond exist or not?

The sky of the Universe, the living original existence of Truth, existed before you were born in the world. This existence exists when you and everything in the world are alive and it still exists even when you and the world disappear. Compared to this existence, the dream that man is in lasts for a split second, and for his life, he lives in a dream having turned away from the origin. Dying is discarding one's self who dreams as well as discarding the places and the content of the dream.

When one removes all of his life in the dream from the Universe, he can go back to the origin. If he is reborn from this origin as the Soul and Spirit of the origin, he can know the world beyond and all the ways of the world.

All material things come from the origin and go back to the origin. This is Truth. The world and the people born in the origin will live forever. He who does not die while he is living will end up dying forever because his true soul does not exist in the land of Truth. Until now, everyone ended up dying and no worlds existed after death. Hell is one's false mind and it does not exist.

If you die while you are living, you will know whether or not the world beyond exists. Now is the age when the world beyond does exist. The world beyond, namely, the true world, exists for one who by killing his self, is born into it and his self who lives in the world beyond also exists.

What Is Heaven And What Is Hell?

In the Bible it says that God and heaven are within you. In the Buddhist sutras it says that your mind is Buddha and that paradise is inside your mind. These sayings seem to have different meanings but they actually mean the same thing. According to Buddhist beliefs *Shakyamuni*, Buddha, resides in paradise. Christians believe heaven is the kingdom where Christ resides. Christ and Buddha are the real, living existence of Truth. They are not false. When we look at a person we see only his outward appearance but a person who has become Truth sees whether or not the person has become Truth. It is possible to know whether one is either alive or dead by the extent to which he has become Truth. His worth will also be measured in the same way.

Man believes he is living in the world, but the reality is that he is living in the mind world he has made. He is dead because he is not living in the real world. Man does not know whether the world of his mind is the real world or not, because his mind overlaps the real world. From the true world's perspective man has always lived and will continue to live inside the false picture world made by his false self.

If one dies while living his life inside that false picture world, he will die forever as a false image inside the false world he has made. However, if one completely destroys the false picture world, and returns to the mind of the origin, the source of the Universe, the world that is reborn within that mind of the origin is heaven and paradise.

This true world is heaven. It is wrong to think that there is another world other than this world. When you discard your false self and your false mind, and you also discard all material existences in the Universe, doesn't the origin become apparent? The land that is reborn as the substance of the origin is heaven and only the master of heaven can accomplish this rebirth.

This land is a living land; an ever-lasting, never-changing land; a true land without death. In this land the self that is comprised of human conceptions and habits does not exist and because one is reborn with the mind of the Universe's substance, he has no worries or anxieties. It is the land of freedom and liberation; the land of God's consciousness. The one who becomes Truth while he is living will have God reborn in heaven, in his mind; and therefore God in his mind will live forever, even after his body passes away. Only a person whose mind has become the mind of the origin of the world can enter heaven and only he can live forever.

The Existence And Non-Existence Of The Soul

Many people are interested in whether or not they have a soul that exists after they die. In the Bible, it states that those who do not believe in Jesus will die forever, and go to hell. However, if one's true soul has been reborn, this soul exists, while one's false soul, or the fake soul seemingly exists, but does not actually exist. It is just an illusion, a picture. It is falseness that wanders around in its own delusions; it is falseness and not true, so it is non-existent.

One is able to live forever when his soul has been born in the true land within him while he is living. In other words, one whose true self has been born in his mind that has become true is able to live forever.

A person who has been absolved of all his sins and has become Truth while he is living will live forever. This is because he has been born in the true land and his soul has been resurrected. However, he who has not been born in the land of Truth will eternally die. One whose soul has been resurrected in the true land inside his mind while he is living has a soul. He who has not become Truth does not.

It Is Not The Material Body That Lives Forever, But The Soul

Nothing that is material in the world is eternal. The sun, the Earth, the moon, and all the millions upon millions of stars in the sky are material entities. Scientists estimate that stars have life spans ranging from five to fifteen billion years. At this very moment, there are some stars in the sky being created and some disappearing. Everything that is material in the world is the origin, the sky before the sky or the original foundation. It is the place of absolute emptiness - when everything in the Universe that one thinks exists is taken away. All material things come from and return to this place. This is the way of the world and Truth. Because all material things have a life span, there is nothing that is everlasting.

Heaven, or paradise, refers to the world where this world has been born in the land of the origin. Only this land is Truth and does not disappear. There is no eternal place unless one is reborn in this land as the elements of Truth. The word *eternal* is only applicable to the land of Truth.

Some religious sects believe that man and the world can live forever, but this is because they do not understand the true meaning behind the religious scriptures. They think that to live forever means man can live in this land eternally as a material existence. However, only the soul that has been reborn in the land of the Creator that is this land, can live forever. Once again, the fact that anything that is material eventually disappears is Truth and the law of the world. Coming from the origin and returning to the origin is the way of the world. The land of the origin, of Truth, is heaven. When one believes Truth, becomes Truth while living, and is reborn in the land of Truth, then he can live forever in this land where the true world exists.

Although many people are curious about where they go after they die, if one is not reborn as the elements of Truth he will die because he does not have the soul of Truth. When one actually repents instead of talking theoretically and he is reborn in heaven, he will come to understand all the ways of the world. One will know Truth as much as he has repented, as much as he has become Truth - this is enlightenment. When one becomes Truth, he will know the principles of the world. However if he just reads the words of Truth without knowing their true meaning, he will think his understanding is correct but he will die forever. If one changes his way of thinking and goes to the place where one can become Truth and truly becomes Truth, he will know that the true soul is the true everlasting never-dying immortal.

Truth knows both Truth and falseness, but the false self knows neither. The false self does not know the true meaning of the holy writings and just interprets them with his human mind.

Thus he cannot know or understand their true meaning. There is nothing higher, more supreme or more perfect than becoming Truth. Therefore, if one achieves completion by becoming Truth, he will know all the laws of the world.

The Way Of The World

The place this world came from is the original foundation, and the place it will go back to is also the original foundation.

Everything in the world is able to exist because the ground exists. The ground is able to exist because the Earth exists, and the Earth is able to exist because the empty Universe exists. The pure empty Universe, that has not one material thing, is the original foundation and the place of Truth. All creations came from this place - think of the place that remained after the animals and vegetation that existed in the world thousands of years ago disappeared - which is the original foundation. This is the place of Truth and the origin of the Universe.

It is the same when people die. Coming from and going back to the origin is the providence of nature, the way of the world and Truth. The world can be saved and people can live only when they are born as the substance of the origin in the place of the Creator, that is the original foundation. All people, animals and plants go back to this place at the end of their life spans.

What does not exist in this world does not exist. Namely, the world that man has stored in his mind by copying everything in the world does not exist. That world is hell. It does not exist because it does not exist in the world which is Truth. Without throwing away this false picture world that is hell, no one is able to go to heaven. Heaven is the original foundation of the world; therefore there cannot be everlasting life or eternity without being reborn in this place as this substance which is Truth. This place, heaven, is where man and the Universe live forever.

We must go back to the origin and be born in the origin. One goes back to the origin when his self has completely disappeared, and only when one dies and does not exist at all, will he be reborn and resurrected. Just as it is the origin, the Creator, that created all material things in the world, spiritual creation is only possible when done by a person who is the Creator. It can only be done by the master of the world because it is his decision to put the creations that are in his world into the land of *Jung* and *Shin*. It can only be done by him, and only he can save everything in the world. Christianity states that only God can save us, and Buddhism tells us that *Maitreya* or the future Buddha will come to the save the world. They are all referring to the master of the world - the master of the origin.

Dying Is Living And Living Is Dying

The *Mahaparinirvana Sutra*, a Buddhist holy writing, says that in the future, in the world of the future Buddha, *parinirvana* or perfect death can be achieved. *Parinirvana* is to die completely, without holding onto anything. What this means is that one must discard all of the human body and mind. Thus, death means to discard or eliminate.

Death means to not exist. To die a "big" death is to die fully without anything remaining - it is when man kills everything in his mind and discards all preconceptions and habits. This is *parinirvana* or *nirupadhishesha-nirvana* (nirvana without residue). When one dies completely, the original mind, the origin, the mind of the Universe, is revealed. This is the mind of the origin; it is God, Buddha and Allah. This is Truth. When man who is false completely dies, he has the mind of God, Truth. When he is then reborn with the Soul and Spirit of God, he will live forever in heaven - in the world of immortals, the land of Truth.

There is a saying in the Bible that he who tries to die will live and he who tries to live will die. This essentially has the same meaning as the sutra above: once one's false self completely dies, his true self is reborn and lives in his land that is true. So, in order for the true self to live, the false self must die. Man believes that he is alive but as he does not exist in the true world, he is a dead entity.

The only way for people who are dead to live, is to discard their false selves. Falseness must die, if the new, true person is to be reborn and live. People often think that when the Savior comes, their bodies will live forever or the souls of their bodies will live forever. However, they are dead because they do not have the mind of the true world and their true souls have not been born in the true world.

It is nonsense to say that one can truly live, if one has not died and been resurrected while he is living. When one repents his sins, it is the death of his self; the complete elimination of one's self that has turned his back on Truth. Without true repentance that is death, one's false self lives in sin that is the false world. This is not truly living; it is death. Only those who have died completely will live forever in the land of Truth.

Resurrection And Rebirth I

What are you looking for and what are you trying to know and gain?

If you die completely, you do not gain anything or know anything. Your mind becomes the mind of the emptiness itself, where everything has ceased - the mind that has become one with the world. Then the world exists within you, you exist within the world, and the world exists in all creations. The reason a speck of dust and the Earth weigh the same is the world exists inside the speck of dust.

This is the mind that has become one with the mind of God. It is the living mind of Truth and the original foundation. Everything is oneness itself, and because everything is Truth they are all alive. The mind of Truth is alive but it does not have the thought, the mind, that it is alive. It is able to accept all things, so all things exist in this mind. The master of the original foundation and heaven will give us salvation. Salvation is becoming true by discarding one's self. When one's self and the world have completely died, the original foundation remains. Being reborn as the Soul and Spirit of the original foundation is salvation.

Only God can give us salvation and only God can save us. His words are Truth because he is Truth, and it is with his words that he will give resurrection and rebirth. All eggs are eggs, but just as there are fertilized eggs and unfertilized eggs, only those who have the seeds of Truth, which is life, can become an eternal and never-dying immortal. A person who has repented all his sins in his lifetime will return to God's bosom and be resurrected. It is not possible to be resurrected or reborn while one still has a self. Only when one goes to the true world after his false self has been completely eliminated and the master of the true world resurrects him, can he be reborn and live. There is no one in the world that can live without being resurrected as Truth by the words of the master.

He Who Goes To Hell, He Who Goes To Heaven

A house can exist because the ground exists and the ground can exist because the Earth exists. The Earth can exist because the Universe, which is the emptiness, exists. The sun, the moon, and the stars in the sky can also exist because the Universe, the emptiness, exists. The Universe, the emptiness, is the origin, the original foundation, and the master of the whole of creation. The Universe is the master and the Creator that brings forth the whole of the Universe.

Let us suppose that you had never been born in this world. This existence of the origin, the original foundation, existed before eternity, exists now, and will continue to exist after eternity. It existed before you were born, it exists after you are born and exists even after you pass away. If you think that you were never born, then aren't you the origin, the original foundation?

You were born from the origin and started to live in a dream, an illusion. You left the origin, the original foundation, and started living in your mind world. All material creations and people on this Earth that existed ten million years ago, five million years ago, ten thousand years ago, now no longer exist. You, who have left the origin and live in your mind, will also disappear with the passing of the years, as have all material creations and people of the past.

In comparison to the perpetuity of the origin, your dream in the world is equivalent to a split second. In that dream there is a world that belongs only to you - a world of your parents, siblings, spouse, children, ancestors, school, job and home, as well as money, love and honor. That was the life you lived, separated from the origin. From the viewpoint of the origin, you alone dreamt a false dream for a split second. The study of Maum Meditation is completely erasing your whole dream.

Completely discarding this dream and returning to the origin is waking up from the dream. When you are born in the origin and no longer dream, you are born in heaven. Heaven is here, the real world; a place where one whose mind has become that of the true world lives. Living in the dream world is hell, but hell is false and therefore does not exist.

All people are living in the hell world. However man does not know he is living in hell because he does not know heaven. Only he who is born in heaven knows both heaven and hell. When one completely destroys his self that lives in the dream world, the world of human life, and all that was dreamt, only the origin, the original foundation, remains. One who is born here will live forever. Heaven is the true world where everything that is false has been destroyed. Hell is where one lives within his mind holding onto his human life. Only he who destroys the hell world and is reborn in heaven can go to heaven.

Man Tries To Attain Truth Through Possession But Nothing Can Be Attained By Possession

Human life has only taught us to have and possess more. That mind of possession and attachment arises from one's feelings of inferiority. Many seek *dō* - Truth or the Way - not for the purpose of becoming a true saint but to use what he learns from *dō* to earn money or to trick ignorant people into thinking that they are great.

However *dō* is not about possessing or attaining; it is about discarding. Discarding one's false self and becoming true is *dō*. A person who tries to possess things is foolish for he will not be able to possess anything; and he who seeks is also foolish for he will not be able to find what he is seeking. Rather, such a person will add to his burdens and suffering eventually leading to a mental breakdown. For someone who achieves something through gain or possession, his achievements reside in his false self.

The more one discards what is in his mind, the more Truth will enter his mind and the more he will be able to know Truth. If he continues to discard, and discard again, all of one's desires - to become great or to achieve something - which arise from his feelings of inferiority will vanish. He will then be able to go to the world beyond these minds - the land of God - and everything that he had desired in the world will all be fulfilled.

Fulfillment or achievement comes from casting off all of one's preconceptions and habits; it does not come from giving in to the greed of one's feelings of inferiority. This only leads to committing more sins and such a person ultimately becomes possessed by greed.

Possession

Possession is the birth of another false self inside one's false mind. There are people who claim they came from heaven, that they are\ the Supreme Being, or the daughter of the Supreme Being, but they were just hallucinating from within their mind worlds. In order for their claims to be true, they need to have come from the original foundation - the original heaven - but their claims are false because they came from their own mind worlds.

When people say that they can see heaven, what they see is the heaven of their minds; it is false because they have made the true heaven into a heaven of their own false minds. Possession is when within the world of pictures that one has taken, a delusion of that world is born again.

When I first spread the words of Truth in Mount Gaya, I allowed many people to see heaven. However, they still had their own mind worlds so as soon as they saw heaven they took a picture of it in their mind worlds and lived within it. I stopped showing heaven to people because I realized that they would speak about heaven from within their mind worlds only a day after they saw it. Because they had a false heaven inside their mind worlds, not only did they speak nonsense, they were unable to truly discard themselves and eventually died trapped within their minds. Almost no one who saw heaven was able to finish this meditation. They died forever.

Possession happens when a person who acts reprehensibly, or rather his deviant hallucinations, tries to compensate for his feelings of inferiority in his mind. Such a person is one who believes in his false self more than Truth, and does not accept Truth; he is a sinner amongst sinners. In Korea it is said that those who foretell the future have many sins. Instances of being possessed by shaman gods or suffering from "spirit sickness" happen when one goes from the false human mind into another fantasy world. Such a person is far from Truth and the ultimate sinner.

This happens to one who deceives his original heart - his original mind or heaven. Truth is not about knowing things in people's lives. He who speaks as if he knows things or foretells the future is speaking nonsense but he who is Truth knows all through wisdom. One who has the original mind of the Universe - a person who has come to his original senses - has wisdom.

The God Of One's Delusions, Omnipotence And Omniscience

The common perception of God is that he exists in some kind of form and shape in heaven. However the existence of God, the origin, can be understood in the following way: When all creations in the Universe are erased, the empty sky remains. When even this empty sky is erased, there is an existence that does not ever disappear. This existence is the source of the Universe; it is the Creator and the existence of Truth; the existence of the Holy Father and the Holy Spirit. It is the origin of the Universe, and it is this existence that is God.

This existence created the Earth, stars, sun and moon in the sky, as well as all creations on Earth. Such is the reason God is said to be omnipotent, because he created every shape and form in the world. All things were created through their surrounding conditions, and by the universal order of God. Creation happens of and by itself, but it can also be said that God, the original foundation, created them. God is omnipotent because he creates, and all creations appear.

God or Buddha is Truth and the original foundation. One can know all the ways of the world when he has become this perspective, which is why God is said to be omniscient. Omnipotence is the power to create the whole world and omniscience is knowing everything about the world. Man will know God and understand what omnipotence and omniscience truly mean when his mind, his consciousness, becomes one with the world.

When God, the Savior, comes to the world he will take man who is living in sin to heaven that is the land of God, and through his words he will give him resurrection and rebirth. This is another instance of God's creation. In the Korean book of prophecy, *Jung-gam-rok*, it is said that a Savior, a saint, must come to the world. In Buddhism, it is said that *Maitreya* must come in order for paradise to be fulfilled on earth. These mean that such an existence will change man's mind from the false human mind to the mind of God and the world; and he will give man rebirth with the body and mind of the origin and Truth within his mind that has become one with the world. This is what salvation is - it is when man becomes reborn as Truth. God gives salvation with his words. It is with his words that he will resurrect man and the world, in man's mind that has returned to the origin. This is only possible when the master of the world has come.

Until now, every religion only spoke of Truth and we only added to our minds and tried to gain and get more. When the Savior comes, people will become Truth and live forever. In the same way that we cannot love our enemies no matter how many times we are told to do so, we cannot become Truth just by hearing about it. We can become reborn in the world of Truth only when we change our human minds to the mind of the world.

This is the only way to live forever and it is the only way to become Truth.

Up to the present Truth was just spoken of, but now anyone can become Truth by subtracting the human mind. The past was an age of adding to one's mind, but now through Maum Meditation one can become Truth by subtracting what is in his mind, and live reborn as Truth. The greatness of Maum Meditation lies in the fact that the hopes of all religions and all people can be achieved.

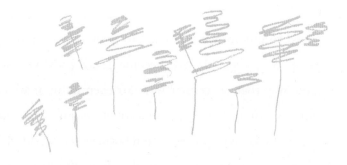

Do Not Be Fooled
For Man There Is No Afterlife
Man Disappears After Death

While people often perform rites of passage to heaven for the dead, and believe that they will receive salvation from their religion, if one does not receive salvation while he is alive he cannot be saved after death. He ends up dying an eternal death or in other words, he dies because he does not have the true Soul and Spirit.

Man is false and incomplete; therefore salvation is when man becomes true, real and complete. Salvation is being reborn in the land of the Creator that is the origin and Truth, with its Soul and Spirit. Salvation is when the world and man are reborn and live in the land of the origin that is God, with the origin's *Jung* and *Shin*, that is otherwise called the Holy Father and Holy Spirit or *Dharmakaya* and *Sambhogakaya*.

Man lives in a false world because not only has the human mind copied everything in the world, he himself lives in this copied world. He is false and incomplete because he lives in an illusionary world and has turned his back on God and Buddha. A person who does not become complete is living in a false and fake world; a person who is living in a world that does not exist also does not exist, so he ends up dying forever. This is what hell is.

Having the pictures of the world that one has made in him is hell. Hell is pictures and it is a copied world; it is non-existent and dead. Man is dead because there is no one who is born in the world of the righteous.

There is no place more beautiful than the world that the Creator, God, has made, and this world is heaven and paradise. However heaven and paradise is overlapped by the mind world of man who lives within his mind world instead of heaven. Therefore, he is dead. He is dead because he lives without knowing the reason or purpose for living and he is not born in the righteous, complete world.

Man can live when he denies his own world and his very self. Then he can return to the world which is the land of God and Buddha; and by the will of the master of the world be reborn and resurrected, and live in the world of Truth. This is salvation.

A Miracle

Many people live hoping for a miracle to happen. There are some people who seek miracles out of their feelings of inferiority in order to appear superior. A miracle is something coming into existence from non-existence; when something that is impossible is made possible; and when what is dead is brought to life. In the world, we often see tricks that look like a miracle, but they are just sleight-of-hand, a trick of the eye.

Although it may appear as though there have been many miracles in the world, a true miracle has never come to pass. A true miracle is when falseness is made into Truth, and when dead people are made real so that they are born and can live. Only this is a true miracle. People are cured from their illnesses when falseness is chased out of their minds and their minds are filled with Truth.

One can be cured of his illness when he ignores his self and has faith in his mind of the existence that is real; ultimately, illness and disease disappear when one discards his false self and only the true mind remains. I have on numerous occasions heard of people who have recovered from their illnesses through Maum Meditation but I do not teach Truth for the purpose of curing illnesses - I find such news inconsequential. My purpose is for false people to recover their original nature in order that they may live a life of nature's flow and go to an eternal world without death where they can be reborn with the Soul and Spirit.

Man is only able to see the outward form and he does not have Truth so he is unable to see Truth that is life. Inside his own mind, he judges whether something exists or does not exist, whether something is dead or alive but that judgment is only his own mind. What is truly alive is Truth, and falseness is dead.

When all material things are eliminated from the Universe, only the empty sky, the origin remains. This origin is Truth and the master of the world. Only a person who is this existence can enable man to be reborn with the body and mind of this existence. The miracles that people speak of are miracles of human affairs, but a real miracle is saving people into the world and allowing them to be reborn in the world with the body and mind of the origin. This is the miracle of miracles - a true miracle. The miracles of human affairs are false miracles. They are meaningless and it makes no difference whether or not they happen.

Only birth in the true world and eternal life are miracles of the world and not a miracle of human affairs. Man pursues Truth to try to find something and attain something. He tries many different things, but what he attains is gained in his false mind. This only adds to his burden and is not true attainment. Living well in the human world and attaining everything that one wishes cannot be achieved from a particular place. If one subtracts what is in his mind a miracle takes place and everything he wished for becomes fulfilled. Everything in God's mind, the mind of the world, becomes fulfilled. The solution is to know that one's regret and bitterness from his unfulfilled wishes are false and futile and to become free from everything.

What Man Is Mistaken About

Man lives in a world of his own mind; therefore he regards the information stored in his mind from childhood through his eyes, nose, mouth and body to be correct. Anything that is not in his mind is often rejected and denied.

Long ago, Korea had its own religion. When Buddhism entered the country it was not well accepted because it spoke of new things. *Chadon Lee*, the Buddhist martyr, was executed. Eventually Buddhism was accepted as the state religion during the period of the Three Kingdoms, and in the *Joseon* era, Confucianism became widespread. Christianity is now prevalent in modern times, but it too was oppressed when it first entered the country.

It is hard for those who are zealous to accept something different from their way of thinking. Even now, every individual has his own religion. Each person thinks that what he believes is right and cannot easily accept what others believe. This is the way of the human mind.

It is also very difficult for people to accept something other than what is within them. In Israel, for example, the followers of Judaism do not believe in Jesus. In each country, a new religion is always oppressed and around the world there have been countless religious wars, which took the lives of innumerable people. The Jewish people believe that the Messiah will come to the world; while the followers of Christianity believe in the second coming of Christ, who is the omniscient, omnipotent God. Christians are waiting for him to come down on clouds accompanied by trumpeting angels. They believe this quite literally without understanding the true meaning and are awaiting the arrival of God in this manner. There are so many different interpretations because there is no one who knows the existence of God, the Truth.

God is the empty Universe itself, the Universe where all material things in the world have been subtracted. This is the original form of God. If this existence comes as a human-being, he has come from heaven because he has heaven within his mind. He is one born as the Holy Spirit; so if God comes in human form, God is human. While man believes that an existence other than a human-being will come, a person who has the land of God within his mind and has the soul of this land itself is Truth born in the original heaven, though he may have the form of a human-being. Even if such a person is living presently among the people of the world, no one would recognize him because in the eyes of man, he is just a man.

The word *omniscient* in the phrase "omnipotent and omniscient", means to know the ways of the world. Man only knows what he has read and learned but if he becomes God, the great Universe, he will know all the ways of the world. Only the Universe knows the origin of human existence; where man comes from, why he lives and where he goes. Man however, does not know.

The word *omnipotent* in that same phrase means the creation of everything in this world is done by God, the origin. This means that everything came from the origin; everything in this world was created by God. God is omnipotent because he created all the billions upon billions of things that exist.

It is through his words however, that God will give new birth to man and everything in the world as the Holy Spirit. This is also why God is omnipotent. Man believes that accomplishing miracles or something of that nature is omnipotence, but a person who saves incomplete and dead people by making them true is omnipotent. Only this person can resurrect the world in the land of Truth and save the dead consciousness of man, giving him life. God, who is omnipotent and omniscient, gives birth to the world in heaven, the land of God; therefore he is omnipotent. Omnipotence is enabling the whole to be born and live.

Material creation occurs when certain conditions come together in balance and harmony that enables the creation. God enables those material things to live forever through spiritual creation. This is accomplished by the word of God, which is his will and Truth. True omnipotent ability is spiritual creation and only God can do this.

Instead of waiting for the coming of his own preconceived notions of a Savior, *Maitreya*, *Jung-do-ryung* or God, man should seek out a place where human completion is possible, as this place may be a sign that the existence of Truth has come. Do not expect this existence to be of a particular shape or form. If a place for becoming Truth exists, then the time for accomplishing Truth and completion has come. A Savior of your own preconceptions, in the form you are expecting will never come. Just as the Jewish people are still waiting for their Messiah, you will wait forever.

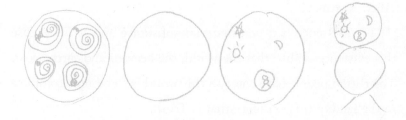

The Essence Of The Universe

The Universe is infinite and it has no beginning or end. The Universe always existed and its origin is the emptiness - the sky before the sky. All of creation came forth from this existence. It is not material; in fact, in this existence there is absolutely nothing yet it is alive and divine because it consists of the one God and Emptiness. It is the semblance of omnipotent and omniscient Truth. Everything in this Universe is this existence itself that has come into form. It is an omnipotent entity and if one becomes the consciousness of this existence then he is omniscient, as he will know all the laws of the Universe. It is because this existence exists that we have the capabilities of the origin, commonly called "instinct".

This existence is a non-material substance and it is because this existence is alive that the world, the heavens and earth, exist. The reason people have come to this world is to become complete in the land of this existence that is Truth.

It is the way of the world that all creations come from this existence and go back to this existence. In other words, coming from and returning to the origin is the way of the world and being reborn in the land of this existence and living, is eternal life and heaven. The core of all religions is about being born and living in this place.

This Universe is alive and only when this existence has come as a human-being can there be salvation, resurrection and eternal life.

The Meaning Behind: Maitreya Shall Come From Paradise And The Messiah Shall Come From Heaven

In the Buddhist sutra, *Mahayana Mahaparinirvana*, it says that man shall be completely enlightened and that he shall know the four states of nirvana - *nitya* (eternal), *sukha* (blissful), *atman* (the self) and *subha* (pure) - when *Maitreya* comes and that *Maitreya* shall come from paradise. This means that one who comes from the place of the origin and Truth in human form as the embodiment of this place, is *Maitreya*. In Christianity, it is said that God shall come from heaven. The heaven mentioned here is also the heaven of the origin; the heaven of Truth; the heaven of heavens, and it also refers to an existence of this place coming in human form.

The references of these two entities may sound different but indicate the same existence. Only this existence can give salvation; thus Buddhists believe that they will be saved when *Maitreya* comes and Christians believe that man can only be saved when God comes down from heaven. Salvation is the complete eradication of this world (called the *"saha* world" or the "earthly world" in Buddhism, and "the world of sin" in Christianity) and the rebirth of one's self in paradise, the kingdom of heaven.

However, no one will know when this existence has come to

the world because man only sees outward appearances. It is only possible to recognize that such an existence has come if heaven or paradise exists in one's mind. But the human mind is one of karma and sin; the existence of Truth and the original mind does not exist within it. Therefore, only when one has completely repented his karma and sins, will he know that *Maitreya* or God has come and be saved. The Savior that people are waiting for - the Savior of their fantasies - will never come.

Only those who have been absolved of their sins and karma and who has Buddha or God in their minds, will know the coming of the Savior. When this existence has come as a human-being, he will teach and guide man to be enlightened of *Mahanirvana Paranirvana* and the four states of nirvana by cleansing their karma. In other words, not only will he teach and guide people to be enlightened of the place of origin, the true self, and the life of heaven, he will also enable them to go to heaven.

When God comes, he will resurrect man who is living in the world of sin, into the land of Truth by cleansing him and eradicating the world of sin as well as the sinner. When the sinner is dead, he is born in the land of Truth; this is resurrection and rebirth. God, Buddha and the land of Truth exist in one's mind only when his mind has become one with the existence of Truth. Only this land is eternal and enabling one to be born in this land is something only the master of this land, the Savior, can do.

Life

Life is to be alive and it is the existence of Truth where the Soul and Spirit that is the origin of the world is alive. Life is an existence that is alive, yet no one knows what life is because man has never learned about life and also because life does not exist within the mind of the self.

The mind of man resembles the mind of the world. The world is life itself, but man's mind, which merely resembles the world, does not have life. In other words, man has taken pictures of everything in the world and stored those pictures in his mind. He lives within that mind that is a copy of the living world; therefore he does not know the origin of life. Only this life is the eternal, never-changing living existence and all material things that are born in this world are an expression of this life. All these things are alive because life that is the origin is alive. Coming from this life that is the origin, and returning to this life that is the origin, is the law of nature; it is Truth.

When people speak of material things being "alive" or "dead", they are speaking from their human preconceptions, from the human mind. Only man is truly dead. Man is not alive because he is an illusion that has departed from the place of life and he is living in a world of his own mind, which does not exist. A camera takes pictures of the world and it produces something that resembles the world. Just as those pictures are not real, man moves, breathes, speaks and eats just as a person in a video does but none of it is real. Man talks about himself from within his own mind world, and his life's fate is determined by the pre-programming that is his mind world. Thus he lives out his life according to the script of his video. What one sees in a video is another world that does not exist in this world; human life is the same.

Everything produced in a video has life only when it exists in the world. Likewise, man must exist in the world in order to have life. The origin of life is the great Universe; the place before all material existence comes forth, the empty sky without material things, the Creator, the origin of the great Universe. This existence itself is the origin of life, so true life is when man returns to this origin and changes his human mind to the mind of the world that is the origin, and is reborn in that world. Discard the mind that resembles the origin and become the origin; only then will there be life. It is the same principle as discarding the videotape, for everything in the videotape is an illusion, and when it has been discarded the world of reality exists and one's self that is living becomes real. Maum Meditation has the method for people to discard this videotape and to be born and live in the world.

The Existence That Is God And Buddha

Jesus Christ taught us that God is within your mind. Buddhism also tells us that Buddha is in your mind and also that you are Buddha. These teachings are talking about the origin - the essence, the source, and also the master of the world. This existence is the Creator that governs the whole of creation and the world but man does not know this existence of Truth. It is impossible for man to know this true existence because it does not exist in the human mind. It remains in one's thoughts and preconceptions as an eternal riddle.

The human mind is a false picture made from pictures taken of the world. Because man has these pictures in his mind, he does not have the true mind so he is unable to see the existence that is true. A block of wood, for example, does not have the mind of pictures. If there is a block of wood in empty space, the emptiness of that space remains unchanged; when it exists, the emptiness is within it, and even when it does not, the emptiness still remains. Likewise, by cleansing his human mind, man can become one with the original essence of the Universe and be able to know God and Buddha.

The human mind is self-centered. By duplicating the world, man makes his own world and he sees and thinks from inside this illusionary, self-made, world. Man is under the delusion that he is living in the world but he is living in his mind that overlaps the world and is therefore unable to know, see or hear the real world.

Buddha and God is the world before this world. Man knows only as much as is in his mind so only he who has the true world can know the laws of the world that is God and Buddha. Simply put, man does not know the world but the great Universe knows it completely. When one returns to the mind of the Universe he will know everything - the laws of the world, where we came from, why we live, and where we will go. He will know heaven and he will also know that man is a false, unrighteous, useless existence who is in fact, dead.

Man thinks something is right if it agrees with his conceptions and habits and if it does not agree, he thinks that it is wrong. However because all human preconceptions and habits are pictures and false, none of his judgments are right - the human mind itself is falseness. This is the reason Jesus Christ said there is no righteous person in the world; the reason Buddha said the human mind is false and human life is futile; that it does not, truly does not, exist.

It is the law of the world that man comes from the origin and returns to the origin. Because man wanders around in his own mind world, his world is a false one that does not exist - it is hell. The reason man lives is to go to heaven while living but instead he devotes himself to his false self living in a false world. Without having done or achieved anything and with only futility remaining, he dies forever with pain and burden. Man must go to heaven while he is still living. Whether or not he is able to do so is a matter of life and death for he only has one life. He may think that he is alive, but this is just his own thought and is not reality because his self is an entity that does not exist.

A wise person will try to know the ways of the world and live forever while a foolish one will not try and die forever. Unless your mind becomes one with the Creator that is the source and origin of Universe, namely, eternal Truth, you will die. Without going back to the beginning, there is no choice but to die as only the origin is Truth.

The existence that is the beginning is the existence of the Creator. It is the true, eternal, and immortal God. It is the Soul and the Spirit of the origin of the Universe. This existence is the eternal Truth, God, Buddha, and Allah.

The Mind

Man is born into the world as the child, the offspring, of incomplete humans and as such, is not a "clean slate" but has human minds from birth. Such inherited human minds are called "original sin" in Christianity. What is referred to as "actual sin" is the world that one has made himself by taking pictures of the world and storing them in his mind. It is also the preconceptions and habits, which are emotions from the picture world that have become one's mind.

Everyone believes that only he is right. This belief comes from the many things he has in his mind. However these things are not real but pictures; they are all false. Everyone living in this world is living in a picture world, and consequently man does not know that he is living in a fake world. He mistakenly thinks he is alive and that he is living in the world because his individual mind world overlaps the real world. However, because he lives in his own mind, he is dead. Only he who is born in the true world knows that all people living in the human world are false.

The true world is a world that is beyond one's mind world, where his self and mind world have been completely eliminated. It is an eternally living world, without death. The origin of Truth remains once everything that exists in the world is gone. In other words, if one discards all forms in the Universe and one's self is also dead and gone, the place that remains is the place of the Creator, the place of the original body and mind. This existence is not material so people think it does not exist but it undoubtedly exists and it is a living existence that does not disappear. Only this existence is Truth. Unless man is born as this existence, the word *eternal* is not applicable to man, and it is not possible to live forever.

Everything in this world is a representation of this existence. The law of the world is that all creations come from and return to this existence that is Truth. The only way for man and the world to be saved is to be born again in the land of this existence. Because this existence is Truth, there is no other way to live eternally.

If one is living in his mind world, it is a fake world that is hell. If he is reborn in the world of God, Truth, the true world, and lives there, it is heaven, eternal life and resurrection. He, who while he is living is born and lives in this land without death, has been resurrected and born into the true heaven. Only he who has gone to heaven while he is alive, lives in heaven.

Heaven is not some place that exists in a certain place. It is within the mind of one whose mind becomes Truth; one who is reborn as the material of Truth. For a person who is resurrected within himself, and lives following the will of Truth, it is his resurrected self that lives and for a person who lives following his own human will, his false self lives and God within him dies. It is the same with glory. If one gives all the glory to Truth, one's self that has become Truth lives, and if one keeps all the glory for his individual self, it is the illusionary ghost that lives.

The greatness of Maum Meditation comes from the fact that it has the method to discard one's false mind. Through this method one can become the true mind, be reborn as the substance of Truth and live eternally. During the time of incompletion Truth was only talked about and no one was able to become Truth. No matter how precious Truth is, if one cannot become Truth, if he cannot become complete, it is utterly useless. Each religion tells us to cleanse our minds - that the poor in spirit are blessed for they will inherit the kingdom of heaven. The place where one can actually achieve this is Maum Meditation.

It is no longer the age of incompletion; it is the age of completion when man can become complete. Even though a method to become complete and go to heaven exists, a person who ignores Truth and does not follow the method due to his faulty way of thinking will end up dying forever. Only when one becomes Truth and lives within Truth, does he have freedom and deliverance. He is an existence we have only heard about until now - a true saint.

Part 3

God's World Beyond
The Human World

God's world is the world of reality,

God's world is a real world.

God's world is a world that exists,

God's world is one that is alive.

From The Age Of Talking About Truth To The Present, The Age Of Becoming Truth

The Bible and the Buddhist sutras are two of many holy scriptures that have been written through the ages. Although the languages and the expressions in these scriptures are all different, they convey the same idea. They speak from the perspective of the origin, the place of Truth, and not from the mind world of man. Man does not understand the words of the living world that is the origin, because he lives in his own mind world. He listens to what is being said from within his mind world and interprets it in his own way. As a result, each religion has split into many different sects. As this happens, the core essence of the religion disappears. Holy scriptures were interpreted to suit people's conceptions and many sects adapted their conceptions to suit the way they are living, until finally, it became a time when Truth was completely modified to suit people.

The time when we only listened to words of Truth was the time of incompletion. No matter how much we listened to the words of holy saints, were we able to become Truth and complete? The only way for man to be able to live is to be absolved of all of his sins and karma, become complete and be reborn. The reason man is incomplete is he does not live in the land of the master and has committed the sin of betrayal by making his own world through duplicating what belongs to the master. This world is a world of illusion. It is now the time when anyone can become true by repenting his sins. Only through repentance is there salvation and it is now the time to go to the land of Truth by becoming Truth.

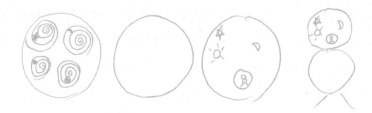

Let Us Find Heaven And The Origin Of Truth Inside Ourselves

In the Bible it says that man was created to resemble God. This means that man was created to only resemble God, not as God himself. Man takes pictures of the physical forms of God that is the true world, and stores these pictures inside his mind. If one takes a picture of the real world that exists, that picture resembles the world but it is not real. Likewise, one's mind is false because it is made by taking pictures of the world, the land of God; it might resemble the real thing but it is false. When one throws away the human mind within his self that is false and his human mind becomes the originally existing mind that is real, the world that is true exists inside man's mind. This world is heaven, and Truth which is God and Buddha exists in one's self.

In other words, a person who has Truth inside him knows Truth and also knows heaven. When man discards his own mind and his mind becomes real by repenting, he becomes the true world and he can be born and live in heaven while he is living.

Salvation Is Not Your Self Living

What is salvation and why do people need to be saved? It is the way of the world that all creations come from the original foundation and return to it. This is the law of nature. Because man is false and an illusion, this falseness must be eliminated if he is to return to the world and be born as a real person. This is man's salvation. Man can only be saved when he is reborn in his mind that has become the world. In other words, only when his false self has completely disappeared can he become real.

The mythical stories of human completion and people living in eternal heaven spoke of the current age: God, Buddha and heaven existing in man's mind when his mind changes from falseness to the real mind of the origin, and then being reborn from the origin. Until now it was the age of incompletion, an age when people read religious scriptures and just talked about Truth; but now it is the age when all people can become Truth and complete, and anyone can become a saint and an eternally living immortal. In the past people only added to their minds. Now people can become complete and live in heaven if they subtract what is in their minds. This is precisely the method of Maum Meditation - it shows you how to discard your false delusions, be born from Truth, and become a true person.

Resurrection And Rebirth II

Resurrection is commonly understood to mean a dead person returning to life. The true meaning of resurrection is the rebirth of the true self after the death of the false self. Man is fake and false because he lives inside his mind, which is a false image. This is the reason there is not a single person who is real and righteous, because instead of living in the world, man is living inside his mind. When the human mind world - man and all material existences in the world - disappears, what remains is the original foundation, which is the source and origin of Truth. True resurrection is the rebirth from the original foundation of one who has become the mind of the original foundation.

The Bible says that no one can live unless he is reborn by the word of God. The Buddhist sutras say that *Maitreya* will save us. Both of these sayings mean that the existence of Truth will enable our souls to be reborn in the kingdom of Truth, and our souls will be resurrected. Resurrection is when the true self is reborn within one's mind that has become the mind of Truth and the original foundation. Resurrection is the death of the false human and the rebirth of the real, true human. Resurrection, salvation, and rebirth all refer to the death of the false self, and the resurrection and rebirth of the true self within a person.

When one completely discards and kills the false self only what is real will remain. Resurrection is when the real body and mind are reborn in the real kingdom, the kingdom of Truth. Resurrection is only possible when you are reborn by the words of Truth. Resurrection and rebirth are only possible when the self completely dies.

The Meaning Of "*Hae-in*" And "Only One Who Has Received The Seal Lives"

Hae-in-sa is a Buddhist temple in *Hapcheon*, South Korea, and in Buddhism *hae-in-sam-mae* refers to a deeply quiet state of mind. Both of these words contain the word *hae-in* (literally meaning "ocean seal") which refers to the kingdom of Truth. The Korean book of prophecy *Jung-gam-rok* says to find the person who holds the ocean seal, *hae-in*, and the ocean seal scepter, *hae-in-bong*. That is to say, those who do not have the seal are all false. However no one knows what the seal truly is. The Bible also states that only he who has received the seal of God will live. The true meaning of "receiving the seal" is the false self and the false world being born into the kingdom of Truth.

To receive this seal, one must repent, become the mind of Truth and one's self and the world must be reborn in that mind of Truth. Only the master, the owner of Truth, can make this happen for only he holds the seal that enables one to be born in the kingdom of Truth. To give the seal of approval means that the false human world is made to exist in the true world.

It also means that the master gives the seal of approval for one to be reborn from the material of Truth in the true world, after the false world is cleansed. The master enables one to live forever because one's Soul and Spirit, *Jung* and *Shin*, is the same as that of the master. The material body and mind will die, but when one is reborn from the origin he has no death because he is Truth. This is why we have to find the person with the *hae-in*; the person who gives the seal of approval.

This existence is the master of the origin, the Creator. Only when this existence comes as a human-being into the world, can he give the seal of approval. Even when a person with the seal exists, man does not know the true meaning of the seal, nor is he able to recognize the person who has and gives the seal; he only thinks of the scriptures he has read in his mind that he interprets through his "common sense"; namely, what he believes to be true. Only when his mind is clean, will he know these things.

Faith

Christianity says that those who have faith in Jesus will go to heaven. While this is correct, people have misinterpreted what it means to believe, or to have faith, in Jesus. Jesus is not a physical shape or an image. Jesus is Truth. Truth is the origin of the Universe, the great Soul and Spirit of the Universe, which is the Creator, God. Jesus had the mind of Truth, therefore believing in Jesus means to be one with, or to unite with, the mind of Jesus. Without believing in Truth, following the words of Truth and repenting, one cannot unite with the mind of Jesus.

In order to be one with the mind of God, the Creator and Truth, one has to throw away his false mind and have the existence of Truth in his mind. This is what it means to truly believe and have faith in Jesus. Man's mind is sinful because each person has his own mind world which prevents him from being one with God, Jesus. When one throws away his sinful mind he will receive redemption from his sins and become one with Jesus - this is faith in Jesus and believing in him.

No one can live without being born as the child of God, by becoming one with the mind of the world of God. Only Truth can do this. True faith is finding Truth by denying and discarding one's own mind and his self. Through death, Jesus united with the mind of God and became the bridge between God and man.

Discarding ourselves for righteousness, like Jesus, should be a matter of course because there is true faith in Jesus only when our minds become the mind of Jesus, of the Creator. When we discard our own individual bodies and minds, our minds become that of Jesus and we have true belief. This is truly having faith in Jesus.

The Level Where One Can Love His Enemies

It is not possible for man to love his enemies unless he is born in the complete land of God.

When doing Maum Meditation, Truth enters one's mind to the extent that he has discarded his false mind, and his enlightenment is equivalent to how much Truth has entered his mind. Enlightenment is knowing Truth. The more he becomes Truth by cleansing his sins, the closer he gets to Truth. When none of his preconceptions and habits remain, and the entity that is his self completely dies and disappears he can get to a level where his consciousness is complete. The level of completion is when one's consciousness becomes the consciousness of the origin and Truth itself. He who is born in this land is Truth and does not die; thus he is a complete person.

One cannot love his enemies just because he has been told to do so. He is able to love his enemies when his consciousness becomes the land of God and when he exists in this land. At such a time, the enemies in his mind will disappear and he will be able to love them. In man's mind world, he is bound to have enemies. Only he who is born in the land of Truth and heaven while he is living is able to love his enemies.

A Person Who Lives By His Own Will Shall Die And The True Self Of A Person Who Lives By The Will Of Truth Shall Live

The Bible teaches us that those who die for God, do not die. What this means is that a person who discards his false self for the sake of Truth will become Truth and live as Truth. The will of a person who is false is also false, and what is false dies. If one discards his false self and lives with the will of Truth then his self becomes God, and it is this self that lives.

He who becomes God while he is living and lives only for God and God's land - a person who sets aside his own will, ignores everything he finds fun and interesting, and puts aside everything he wants to do - will live as Truth, which is God. On the other hand, for one who does as he desires and lives according to his own will, his false ghost will live and God will die.

When, for the sake of God, one discards and sacrifices his self and accumulates blessings in God's kingdom, such everlasting blessings are in God's kingdom and are his. This is the meaning of what is said in the Bible, that fools store their treasures on earth, while the wise store their treasures in heaven.

Love, Compassion And Virtue

The words "I love you" are commonly used between lovers, married couples, parents and children.

However human love is the fulfillment of one's demands. In other words, human love is full of expectations; man cannot love unconditionally. Pure love is giving without the mind of having given. This is true love, compassion and virtue.

Man and all of creation are able to exist because the origin, the empty sky, exists. Although the empty sky creates everything and provides man with food, air and the means to live, it does not expect anything in return. Such is the mind of the origin. True compassion, love and virtue do not exist unless man's mind becomes that of the origin.

The mind that is without the thought that you have done something for someone; the mind that is absent of the thought that one has done anything at all; the mind where the left hand does not know what the right hand is doing - this mind is only possible when your mind becomes that of God. When you chase out your evil, false, self-centered mind and change it to the mind of God, you can live for the world and others.

The human mind that is self-centered does not have love, compassion or virtue; there is only the mind that cares for himself.

While it is often said that we must love our enemies with compassion and virtue, we are unable to do so because enemies exist within the deeply rooted minds we have.

Maum Meditation is the practice of changing one's human mind into the mind of God and becoming reborn as the child of God. Maum Meditation is a place where one can actually become a saint, Buddha, the son of God; the entities about which we have only heard. It is a place where one can achieve human completion.

God's World Beyond The Human World II

People have been in the world for a long time. Man is born in the world through the balance and harmony of creation and the will of heaven and earth enables him to live. However, he lives as he wishes; he makes his own world and believes he is alive because of his own greatness. He does not know he exists because the world exists. He is not thankful for the world and he only acknowledges what suits the framework of his mind; if something does not suit his mind, he rejects it as being wrong.

We need to think about what the source of the world is, that is, what the existence of the origin is. Let us suppose for a moment that we had not been born in the world - the Universe would still exist. If all the stars in the sky that were created by the Universe had never been created, then only the empty sky would exist. This existence, the empty sky, existed before the beginning, exists presently and will exist for an eternity afterward. It is the original foundation that exists of and by itself. It is the eternally living, never-dying *Jung* and *Shin*, the Soul and Spirit, the Holy Father and Holy Spirit, *Dharmakaya* and *Sambhogakaya*.

There is absolutely nothing in this existence but the one God that exists amidst the nothingness. The nothingness is the body of the Universe and the one God is the mind of the Universe.

The word *holy* refers to this existence; it is holy because it is alive and creates all of heaven and earth. It is the way of the world that all creations come from this existence and return to this existence. The Korean euphemism for death, "he has returned" means you return to this existence when you die.

This existence is the origin, the source and the Creator. This existence is the master of the living Universe. This existence brought forth heaven and earth and created heaven and earth. From the viewpoint of this existence man who lives a self-centered life is not living righteously.

Man lives in his own mind and is therefore a sinner who acts against the original foundation, which is Truth and the master of the world. The original form of God is the infinite Universe - the empty sky itself. Man was made to resemble God but he copies into his mind everything in the world that God has created and constructs his own mind world. God is the world that is true, and what man makes is a world of a video - a type of picture. A photograph is a print on paper of what belongs to the world, but man prints and keeps in his mind of what belongs to the world and all that has happened in the world. The place where man is living overlaps the real world and so he mistakenly thinks he is living in the world but he is actually living inside the world of a video. This is his karma and the reason he is a sinner.

God's world is not the human world, but the true world that can be seen. Even though man is born into the world, he has never once lived in the world. When he destroys his mind world and his self disappears, he can go to the world of God, the true world. Beyond the complete destruction of the human world, the illusionary world, lies the true world, the world of God. Man is a sinner and an illusion and when he disappears, he can go to the true world of God.

People follow the words of saints because they are incomplete and there are people all over the world who strive to become saints themselves. However, only God knows the way to get to the land of God and only he can give new birth to those who have come to the land of God.

The world of God is the land where one lives as an eternal immortal. Therefore the Savior must be the master of the world. He will take people to the world of God and enable them to be reborn in this world as well as enabling the world to be reborn in the world of God. In other words, only when everything in the Universe is reborn in the empty sky, the origin, as the substance of the empty sky, can it live eternally like the empty sky.

The human world is a false world,
the human world is a fake world,
the human world is a non-existent world,
the human world is a dead world.
The human world is one without life,
the human world is a world of hell,

the human world is a world of pictures,

and the human world is one of suffering and burden.

But God's world is the world of reality,

God's world is a real world.

God's world is a world that exists,

God's world is one that is alive.

God's world is a world that has life,

God's world is the world of heaven,

God's world is what the pictures have been taken of -

the original form of the world.

God's world is one of freedom and liberation.

The way to go to God's world beyond the human world is by dying and completely destroying one's mind world. Maum Meditation is causing a sensation around the world because it has this method.

Let Us Go To Heaven While Living

In life, we often hear the terms "heaven" or "paradise". In every religion, we hear that those who do good deeds in life will go to heaven or paradise while those who do bad things will go to hell. This is why many people think about whether heaven exists. However, there is no answer from within the human mind world and many try to get to heaven through practicing religion.

The true heaven is not some fantastical place - it is here; it is this world. This world is the true world free from one's mind world. One's mind world - the world made by taking pictures of the world from within one's mind world - is hell. When this world is completely destroyed, it is heaven, which is this world right here. Hell is the illusionary world and heaven is the real world: the world of the true Soul and Spirit, which is the origin of the world.

When a person becomes one with the mind of Truth, the true world, while he is living, he has the world that is the Soul and Spirit of Truth in his mind that has become true. This world is heaven. A person who does not go to heaven while he is living is in a world of hell. Heaven does not exist in hell so he ends up dying. He dies because he is in a world of illusion. One must change his human mind to the mind of God while he is living in order to live in the land of God. Then he is in heaven. If he is to be born and live in heaven, one must become complete while he is alive.

The Plan For Human Completion

Man has tried to achieve completion for a long time through various methods, by practicing asceticism or by following various religions. And although traces of these efforts to achieve completion can be seen and heard everywhere, there has never been a method, or plan, to achieve completion.

When we encounter difficulties in our lives, we often wonder if a mystical method to solve our problems exists. Similarly, becoming Truth has perhaps been the most difficult task in the world because there has never been a method to get to the existence of Truth.

Although there have been countless people in the world, a method for human completion has never existed because the complete existence - the master of the original foundation - had not come to the world. Man has been waiting for this Savior because only this true existence knows the way to become Truth, and can make man become Truth.

The Savior is the one who saves the world. The plan for saving the world is to make man's mind one with the mind of the origin of the world, and to enable man to be reborn in the land of Truth. Only the Savior knows how to do this, because the human mind world does not know the things of the world, Truth.

The systematic, scientific method to erase the false human mind world - to become one with the mind of the real world when one completely erases the false human mind world - is openly available to the public at Maum Meditation. This is the plan for human completion. By completely subtracting and erasing the human mind world, the place of Truth, completion, is revealed. When one is reborn in this world he achieves human completion. Being reborn as Truth is human completion.

Only The Creator, Truth, Can Cleanse Us

Truth knows both what is false and what is true, but falseness knows neither Truth nor falseness. Therefore, no one in the world knows Truth because man is not real but false and incomplete. He is an entity without life and he is a sinner because he makes and lives in his own world that has turned its back on God, Truth. Only Truth can destroy and eliminate falseness and only the master of the original foundation, of Truth, knows the method to do so. In other words, only what is true can eliminate falseness.

During the time of incompletion, many people became ascetics and tried hard to find Truth. However, no one has been able to achieve Truth - if someone had achieved Truth, a method to become Truth would already exist. Because of man's ignorance he does not know that it is nonsense when someone claims that he, and only he, has achieved Truth.

If one has achieved Truth, he must have a plan, a method, for anyone to do the same. A place that enables one to become Truth can do so because it has Truth. Only Truth can enable one to become Truth and only Truth knows what falseness is, and can destroy and eliminate that falseness, and only Truth can resurrect one as Truth. Therefore, Truth is the Creator.

What Would The Savior Do When He Comes?

In Buddhism, it is believed that when *Maitreya* comes he will enable man to become Buddha and take him to paradise and there are Christians who believe that when the Savior comes he will take church-going Christians to heaven. While everyone has a different idea of what the Savior will be like, it is widely believed that the Savior will be kind, compassionate and caring. However, man is dead within his sins and karma and in order to enable him to receive absolution from his sins, the Savior must make man discard what is his and kill his false self. Therefore people may regard the Savior as their worst enemy because of their human preconceptions and habits. The Savior is great compassion and kindness itself and he kills man in order to save him. However he is man's enemy because that which is false tries to become Truth whilst holding onto falseness; man tries to become Truth while holding onto himself.

We need to realize that the Savior is not simply an existence of love, compassion and tenderness, but one who kills your false self. If you are completely dead, the Savior allows you to be reborn in the land of heaven. In order for this to happen, man must discard his ways of thinking, his preconceptions and habits, money, love, fame, family, all that he has, as well as his own self for the sake of righteousness. Consequently, the Savior who teaches this will be man's greatest enemy.

The result of this is that man will be reborn, resurrected, and live forever in heaven. Therefore, the Savior is in fact the embodiment of true love, true affection and great compassion. The Savior makes man cleanse his sins and karma so that he may be reborn in the land of the Savior. The absolution of sin, or the cleansing of one's sin and karma, is when man, who is false and incomplete, escapes from his greed, thereby returning to the origin, the mind of the Savior. Only he who has been absolved of his sins and cleansed his karma will go to heaven and live forever.

What Being Reborn As The Holy Spirit Means

Being reborn, resurrected, and born again as the Holy Spirit, all have the same meaning. When it is said one cannot live unless he is reborn by water and the Holy Spirit, it means man is a sinner and is dead. The water represents the washing away of one's sins; this is the reason some places still baptize people with water. This does not mean that sin is actually washed away by the water; it represents the method with which one can wash away his sins. Man must wash away his sins for the Holy Spirit to be within him. To wash away sin is to eliminate all false minds made by copying the world.

When these sins do not exist, then one becomes God's mind, the mind of the Creator, the origin and Truth. He must become one with the mind of the world, and be reborn, resurrected, from the world. He is reborn as the Holy Spirit when his Soul and Spirit is reborn in the kingdom of Truth.

Man believes that in the true world, he will continue to live as he is. However, while his appearance may stay the same, it is not the false self but his true self that is reborn as the Soul and Spirit of Truth in the kingdom where the self has become one with the mind of the world. This is rebirth as the Holy Spirit. The Holy Spirit is the Soul and Spirit of Truth, which has been reborn. It is to be reborn within one's self, in the world where the mind has become one with the world. He who is born in the kingdom of Truth, beyond the death of the false self becomes the forever-living, never-dying immortal. Therefore, even when his material body disappears, he lives forever.

There is nothing material in this world that lasts forever. All material things come from the origin and return to the origin. This is the way of the world. However, only the master of the kingdom of Truth, through his words, has the ability to give man new birth in the kingdom of Truth, the origin, because he is life itself.

The meaning of being reborn as the Holy Spirit is to be reborn as the soul of the Holy Spirit in the land of the Holy Spirit, which is the origin and Truth, by repenting all of one's sins. One must have the land of the Holy Spirit in his mind while he is living and only he whose true Soul and Spirit is resurrected in the land of the Holy Spirit that is within him while he is living, will live.

This Soul and Spirit exists within you even when your body is alive. It is the child of God who exists in heaven, and so even when the body dies it exists forever, without death. Man must live in heaven, while he is still alive. Only he who has gone to heaven while he is living can have eternal life; one whose mind is the false world is a false person, therefore he will die forever.

We must become real and true while we are living, and be

reborn as the Holy Spirit. Repenting your sins should become the greatest priority, for he who is absolved of all his sins has the true mind and the right to be born in the land of Truth.

Rebirth, resurrection, being born again as the Holy Spirit is the disappearance of one's false mind world and consequently, as the real mind of the world is within his self, one's birth in that land of Truth. Such a person is one who is reborn as the Holy Spirit. When your false self dies and you go beyond your false world, that is, when the false world disappears, what is real remains. Being reborn as the Holy Spirit is to be born in the real world.

The Completion Of The Universe
(The Completion Of This World)

Completion is to be able to live forever and not die. Since the Universe was first created, it has never been complete. The Universe itself, that is, the origin that is the emptiness, is the master. This existence is the living existence of Truth and it created the material Universe. Everything in the Universe was created by the providence of heaven and earth; by cause and by conditions. The law of the world is that material things come from the origin and return to the origin, the master of the Universe. This is also Truth. All material things that disappeared after existing in the world have returned to the origin and none of them exist. This is basic common sense. Coming from the origin and returning to it is Truth.

However, completion of this world is accomplished when all material creations are reborn with the elements of the origin, the original foundation. This is the salvation that all religions speak of, and this is the completion of the Universe. The Creator, the master of the Universe, created the material things in the world, and likewise, when the master of the Universe, the Creator, comes, only this master of Truth who is human can resurrect the world in the land of completion. In the time of completion, the complete person will come to the world and accomplish completion. The coming of the master of the origin as a human-being in this world is referred to in religion as the coming of the Savior. Only this existence, the master of the origin, is able to save the world.

The Master Of The Origin, A Person,
Accomplishes The Completion Of The Universe

The Universe is infinite and without end. The sky before the sky, which is the origin of the Universe and the place of the source, is the original foundation of the Universe and the place of Truth. A house exists because the ground exists, and the ground exists because the Earth exists. The Earth exists because of the sky. All the stars, the sun and the moon, exist because of the sky, which is the origin.

The place of the origin, Truth, is revealed when all material things in the sky, such as carbon or hydrogen in the air, are removed. It is the place of the Soul and Spirit of the Universe, the Creator. It is the place of the Holy Soul and Holy Father, the place of the body of Buddha and the mind of Buddha, the place of *Jung* and *Shin*. The place where nothing exists is the place of *Jung*, the body of the Universe, and amidst the nothingness, one mind, *Shin*, God, exists. The source of the Universe is this existence which is not material. It is the real metaphysical substance and it is alive.

This existence is the Creator, Truth. The Soul and Spirit of this existence that is Truth created all material things in the world. It is because this existence is omnipotent and omniscient that all material things are able to come forth according to the circumstances of the environment. That is to say, when the circumstances are right, all sorts of things are created. "This" exists because "that" exists and therefore "this" also exists and so forth.

Each religion talks about a Savior - *Maitreya* who will come from paradise, God who will come from heaven - who will save the world. What they mean is that the existence of the origin will come to the world as a person, and save the world.

This means that only this existence of Truth, can accomplish true salvation, which is taking people to the kingdom of Truth. Because man has karma and sins, one who discards his karma and sins can go to heaven. The Savior's only role is to enable man to be reborn and live in the world of the Savior, where eternally there is no death. Another way to explain this is that the Creator, the metaphysical real existence of the origin, created the material world and when the Creator, the source of the Universe, comes to the world as a person he will enable man and the world to live eternally in his own kingdom of the true Soul and Spirit, the kingdom of Truth.

The completion of the Universe, the world, and man is when a person who is the master, the origin, the Truth, the Creator, enables the true Soul and Spirit to be reborn and live forever in the kingdom of the true body and mind. This is the completion of the Universe and the one who accomplishes completion is the complete person and Savior. Whether it is material or spiritual creation, it can only be done by the Creator.

The New Sky And The New Earth

In Christianity it is said that those who believe in Jesus will live eternally in a new heaven and earth at the second coming of Christ, while in Buddhism it is said that when *Maitreya* comes people will live forever in the kingdom of Buddha. These two different expressions have the same meaning. Everyone in the world is living in the *saha* world - the world of sin - and not in the new heaven and new earth. However, when the world of sin is completely destroyed, the world of Truth emerges - therefore it is the new heaven and new earth. In order to live there, one must go to the land of Truth and be reborn within it.

There is no place that is more beautiful or more perfect than this world that God created. However man has turned his back on God. He puts into his mind a world created by taking pictures of the world of oneness; this mind world overlaps the world so he is under the illusion that it is the real world. Therefore this picture world is the world of sin.

Taking one who is living in his own mind world to the world of Truth and giving him new birth in this world is salvation. Such a place is also the new heaven and earth. In the land of God, the world itself is already completely saved. Man is not able to go to this world because he lives within his sins and karma so only he who repents his sins can go to this world.

He who tries to accomplish Truth with his false self is not able to do so. People often try to accomplish Truth by themselves once they know the method and there are also those who give up along the way. The study of Maum Meditation is the cleansing of one's false self and false mind in order to become the mind of Truth and be reborn and resurrected in the land of Truth.

Because one's self is false, even if he does accomplish Truth it is false. It is possible to be enlightened of the first few levels from within one's false self but beyond that, each level has a differ- ent method to destroy his false world and it is impossible to get beyond a certain point without these methods. If we assume that Truth can actually be achieved in Maum Meditation, a person who is in the place where it is possible to achieve Truth will be successful but a person who tries to achieve Truth by himself will fail for he has turned his back on the place where Truth can be achieved. In other words, he is trying to achieve Truth when he has turned his back on Truth. Achieving Truth is to become Truth. When one turns against the place of Truth, it is the false- ness within him that is trying to achieve Truth and it is only logical that what is false cannot become Truth.

I have observed that those who do achieve completion are the ones who are thankful for enlightenment and continue to work silently towards completion.

Those who do not reach completion have a lot of karma and

sins. They are unable to overcome their strong frameworks of mind. They are too bound to them, and are therefore unable to escape from them. Only he who repents truly, knowing that his self is false and an illusion, is able to achieve Truth.

The Will Of The Sky

This place, here, is the sky. Up there is also the sky; here, there and everywhere, all of it is the sky.

The whole world is able to exist because the empty sky exists; this is the true will of the sky. It is because of the existence of the empty sky, that the celestial bodies of the Universe and everything on earth are able to exist. Just as we are able to live because the Earth exists, the Earth and all celestial bodies are able to exist, because the empty sky exists. Every material thing in the world is able to exist, because the original foundation exists.

Even if the celestial bodies, all creations and material things do not exist, the empty sky would still exist. Even when they do exist, the empty sky exists of and by itself, inside the material things. It is the way of the world that material things come from the empty sky. When they come into being and then disappear, the empty sky still exists. Again, it is the way of the world that the place we come from and go back to is the empty sky; thus it is to be expected that we become the empty sky after death.

However man makes and lives in his own mind so he is unable to live in the world. He ends up dying because he lives inside his own mind which is a false image he has copied of the real world. When this mind world is erased, he becomes one with the mind of the empty sky. At that time the world and his self are reborn in the empty sky with its Soul and Spirit. There is no one who can live without such rebirth.

The heaven that people think of as being somewhere "out there" is a delusional heaven. It will become an established fact that eternal life is possible only when one is reborn in the empty sky - the truly existing Truth. This is what it means when it is said that those who are born in heaven will live in heaven.

The existence of the empty sky is Truth, God, Buddha and Allah. *Jung* and *Shin*, the Holy Father and the Holy Spirit, *Dharmakaya* and *Sambhogakaya* exist in this existence. In other words, it is a place of complete emptiness, and yet the one God exists within it. The emptiness is the body of the Universe - the Soul - and the one God is the mind of the Universe - the Spirit.

Every material thing in the world is created from the conditions of its environment; in other words, if this exists then so does that, and if that exists then this also exists. The body and mind of the Universe, where all is one, are expressed through material things. The form of the empty sky is every material thing that exists. The empty sky is non-material; a metaphysical essence. This entity is not material but it exists in all material things. Because the empty sky is the Creator, there is nowhere it does not exist.

In order to be born in the sky, that is the original foundation, the Creator and Truth, one must erase his self from the world.

The empty sky must become his mind and he must be reborn as this essence. Only then can he go to heaven while he is living and live eternally. Only the master of the empty sky can resurrect someone in the empty sky. This is salvation itself. Because the empty sky that is alive exists, it is possible for the stars, the sun, the moon, the Earth, everything on Earth and people to exist. This empty sky is the Creator itself and it is only when the master of the empty sky comes as a human-being, that it is possible for the world and people to be born into the empty sky. This is the completion of the Universe. In other words, the completion of the Universe is when all that exists is saved. When the world that was trapped and dead inside man is reborn in his mind, he is the master of that reborn world and as the master, he will gather citizens into that world. That is, he who is born in heaven will live in heaven and do the work of heaven.

The will of the sky is not what people think - the sky exists in a place beyond will, but of and by itself at the right time, Truth forms into action. This is the will of the sky. Now is the time for the world to be born in the sky. It is also the time for your self to be born in the sky. This is the will of the sky and we must go to heaven in this time and live eternally. The reason and purpose we are alive is to be born in heaven and live forever at this time.

The Savior Will Come From The Sky, Maitreya Will Come From Paradise

The sky is often thought of as being far away but when the human mind is one with the sky, it exists within the human mind. When all material forms in the world are eliminated, only the original sky remains. This is the true sky; it is Truth and it is comprised of the Holy Ghost and the Holy Father. The Savior of the world is the existence who is reborn by himself into the land of the true mind and returns to the world.

Many believe that Jesus Christ, who passed away two thousand years ago, will come down from heaven on a cloud in the same physical form he had then. This is neither scientifically nor realistically possible. When we speak of Jesus Christ we are speaking about the existence of Truth. If the existence of Truth comes, then Jesus Christ has come; the Savior has come. When the one whose mind has become the sky - he whose soul is resurrected by himself in the land of Truth - comes into the world, he is the Savior from heaven.

It is also the same for the saying that *Maitreya* will come from paradise. Paradise is the sky among skies; the sky of the original foundation. The one who is reborn as Truth from the mind of this sky - the one who has come again - is *Maitreya* who has come from paradise.

Both of these religious teachings mean that a saint, who is the Truth, will take people to the kingdom of Truth and enable them to live there. Only this existence can save people. This is because only this place is the land of Truth and only he who is born in this place can live forever.

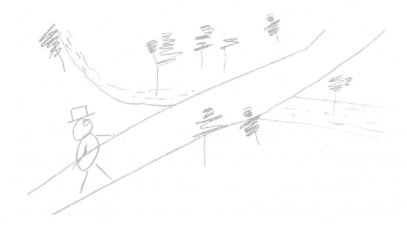

The Words Of Saints

So many people have come and gone in this world but only a few have become saints while the rest have just passed away. Past saints all prophesied that the time of completion would come and that man would be able to go to heaven at that time. For example, the philosophy of the *Dan-goon* era (the era of the founding father of *Gojoseon*) prophesied the coming of a time of unity and prosperity. *Jung-gam-rok*, a Korean book of prophecy, states that in the time of incompletion one should look for *sipseungji* - a haven - on Earth but in the time of completion, one must look for *sipseungji* in heaven. From ancient times there has been a Korean saying that when *Jung-do-ryung* comes it will be possible to become complete. The Buddhist scriptures also foretold the coming of *Maitreya* while the Bible prophesied the coming of the Savior.

All of the above prophesy the coming of the master of the Universe from the origin as a human-being. It is not possible for Truth to be accomplished without the master of the Universe who is Truth coming to this world. The saints of the past could not make man complete; they could only speak about Truth and foretell the time of human completion. The Universe also has seasons; there is a season for human completion and the completion of the world. At this time a complete person will come.

The way of the world is that all creations come from the origin, from Truth, and go back to the origin. In other words, all creations come from the original Universe and return to the original Universe - what comes from nature goes back to nature. This is the way of the world. One has to be reborn and resurrected in the origin that is Truth in order for the resurrected Soul and Spirit to live forever. Such is the completion of the Universe. For the completion of the Universe to come about, a complete person has to come to this world. There is no way for man to live without being born in the kingdom of the Creator, the origin and Truth. All saints predicted the coming of this time of completion.

If there is a place for one to become complete, then it must be the time of completion, but *Jung-gam-rok* clearly states that even in the time of completion, one cannot enter into the season of completion if he is too tightly bound to his religion. Afraid that we may lose the chance for human completion, our ancestors have already given us many hints. In *Jung-gam-rok*, for example, it tells us to find the place where the cow is lowing, or the place where you can cleanse your mind. Even though it tells us in much detail, people still do not understand.

The Era Of Saints

A saint is someone who has the mind of the Creator, Buddha and God, and not the mind of his own self. Furthermore, a true, living saint is one who has been born in the kingdom of Truth - one who has become an eternal, never-dying immortal. Such a person has repented and been absolved of all his sins and therefore he is a person without sin. He has been absolved of his karma and is without karma. He is one who has completely eliminated his false self and his illusionary self of sins and karma; one who has won over his false self and eliminated the world of illusion.

If one becomes a saint while he is living, this land, here, is paradise and heaven. Therefore even when his material body disappears, he is an eternal never-dying God in this land of the Soul and Spirit. A saint is without self; he is one who has become Truth. He builds the land of righteousness and enables people to become righteous. He destroys the world where the devil and ghosts live, and makes the ghosts of that world surrender.

A saint does not live for his self, the ghost, but lives for the people of the world. He saves the dead, false ghosts that live in the ghost world. This world is already the world of the saint and is saved, but a ghost that has self does not live in the saint's world, the true righteous world. Therefore, a ghost needs salvation in order to live.

Now is the time when everybody can live forever in heaven, by changing this land, the ghost world, into the true land through repentance and penitence. It is the era of the saint.

A saint has the righteous kingdom within him. He also has God, Buddha and Allah within him. This land is the heaven amongst heavens, where only forever-living and never-dying immortals live and it is the master of this land who enables one to be born into this land. One who is born into this land is a saint and a complete person. He is one who has become Truth.

The End Of The World Defined

It is commonly believed that "the end of the world" means the world will actually come to an end - that it will disappear. The real meaning of the end of the world is that a new world will come, putting an end to the old world. In the old world people lived with human minds. In the new world, people's minds become that of God and they live reborn as God.

In the old age, man lived in his false mind world but in the new world, the new age, he lives as God in the land of God. So one who is born in the new world will live forever because he lives as God in the kingdom of God. However, for one who dies forever within his own mind, it is the end of the world.

There have always been famines, droughts and earthquakes. There will always be these natural disasters - they will not cause the world to disappear. A person who lives born in the land of God and Truth lives in the new world; a person who lives in his mind world that does not exist in the real world will die forever.

Thoughts On Everlasting Life

Religions tell us that in heaven and paradise, one does not die. In order to live forever, we must be reborn with an eternal body and mind in an eternal place. In the Universe, there is only one place like this. This place is the original root that brought forth the Universe that is the origin and Truth. The original root is the place that has been cleared of all material matter in the Universe; that is to say, it is the place where the celestial bodies in the sky, the earth and one's self do not exist. Doesn't the sky of the Universe remain when all material things in the Universe are gone? This is the place of the Creator, Truth, which is eternal and does not disappear. There is no eternity without being born in this place. If one discards his false human mind and is reborn in this place by becoming the mind of the great Universe then heaven and paradise is this place right here.

Heaven is within the mind of one whose mind has become heaven itself. You can live forever when your mind becomes this true mind and you are born as the true Soul and Spirit inside this mind while you are living. One cannot live in this place unless he discards all material things and his human body and mind; unless the origin, Truth, becomes his mind and he is reborn and resurrected. Only he who has gone to heaven while he is living is able to go to heaven after death because he has heaven.

The Correct Meaning Of Eternal Life

Eternal life means to live forever. To live forever is to never die, and never dying means that one is truly alive. In order to live forever, one must fulfill the prerequisite condition for eternal life - one must become Truth itself. In order to do this, one must completely eliminate all the karma and sins that one has committed. Then, Truth emerges and one can become Truth.

Karma is the sins that one has committed. The sins of man are that he has not become one with Truth, the origin; he has turned against Truth; and he lives within his own mind world. When he is absolved of his sins, returns to Truth, the origin, and is reborn as Truth he will have eternal life. Only Truth lives forever because only Truth is life itself. In other words, man will live forever only when he is reborn as the Soul and Spirit of God, of Truth.

Man unknowingly lives trapped in his world of hell that is sin. From the viewpoint of Truth, this hell world is a non-existing world, a false world of images. Because man lives within this world of false images he is not alive, but dead. Strictly speaking, a person who lives in a non-existing world does not exist. He thinks he exists and that he is alive, but it is the ghost, a false image, thinking it exists and is alive.

This hell world is a non-existent world, a world of death. The real world is alive, and although everything that exists in the world is also alive, only man is dead. He will be able to live when he is reborn as the body and mind of the world. He who is born on the earth will live in an illusionary world of the earth, while he who is born in heaven will live in heaven when he is reborn as the body and mind of heaven.

Although all creations are alive, man is not born in heaven because he has possessed his own mind. Therefore, he will live in heaven when he is "poor in mind". To be "poor in mind" means one has no human minds. When one does not have human minds, he becomes one with the body and mind of the world, and thus death no longer exists for him.

Consider this - the sky existed before eternity, exists now, and will exist after eternity. There is no death when one is reborn as the body and mind of the sky and he will live in the kingdom of the sky eternally. The world is originally completely enlightened and alive but man's mind is not able to become one with the sky and he possesses his own mind which is an act against the sky. Thus the purpose of Maum Meditation is to enable people to be saved, that is, to attain Buddha-hood, by being reborn as Buddha, the Son of God.

Only the Truth can bring forth Truth; and only Truth will live eternally. Maum Meditation is the study of becoming Truth. *Huh, huh, cham* - literally "false, false, truth" - is a Korean expression which means after all the falseness have been erased only Truth remains. A person who lives in his mind world insists that only he is right and others are wrong, but just as Jesus said, there is no one in the world who is righteous; no one in the world is true. Therefore everyone should cleanse his wrongful mind and go to heaven while he is living. Nothing in the world is more urgent or important than this.

Maum Meditation enables people to discard their false minds, to be reborn as Truth and resurrected as an eternally living immortal.

What It Means To Become The King Of One's Kingdom When One Dies

It is said in Christianity that when Christ's followers die they will each be appointed a kingdom over which they will reign. Christ is a reference to Truth - the Creator - and this existence itself is the origin and source. Therefore, one who returns to the origin and is reborn becomes the master of the new land, the new heaven and earth, for he has this world of the Soul and Spirit within him. For each person who is born in the world of the Soul and Spirit where this heaven and earth exists, this true mind world becomes his and he becomes the king of the world of the Soul and Spirit. A king must accumulate citizens and fortune in his world in order for his world to prosper.

What the Bible means when it says that the foolish store their treasures on earth while the wise store their treasures in heaven is that one must store his treasure in the true heaven that is his world in order for it to be eternally his. The basic requirement to go to heaven, paradise, is to eliminate one's own mind and become one with the mind of the source, of Truth, of the world and heaven. Only then does he have the Creator which is Truth within him, and only then, can he be reborn with the body and mind of the Creator.

Man has attachments to his body so he mistakenly thinks that it is his body that lives but the body is an illusion; it is not the true soul. When one has destroyed and cleansed his false body and false world, the origin remains and it is only when one is resurrected from the origin that the world becomes the kingdom of Truth - the new world. This kingdom is inside one's mind and it is a new world because it did not exist before. One is the king or the master of this new world because his dead self has been reborn in that world. A king should build his kingdom by working diligently for his new world.

God's World Beyond The Human World II

The religious terms, "heaven", "paradise", "the world of the Great Jade Emperor" and "the world of the divine hermit" all refer to the true world. This world is the world of God. The human world is one where man receives his body from his parents and turns against the true world from his birth. He comes into this world of sin, betrays the Creator, which is the world and origin, and makes and lives in his own world. This is why man is a sinner. If the false and illusionary human world made by one's self is completely demolished and his false self also completely disappears, he will go back to the original foundation, which is God's world. God's world beyond the human world is where one can live forever without death as an eternally living immortal. It is heaven and "the world of the divine hermit".

If the human world disappears, only God's world remains. The origin and Creator of the Universe is the original foundation. You are able to exist because there is a foundation that is the Earth on which to exist, and in turn the Earth is also able to exist because of the foundation on which it exists - the empty sky. The empty sky is the original foundation. This existence is the living existence which is *Jung* and *Shin*, Soul and Spirit, the Holy Father and Holy Spirit, *Dharmakaya* and *Sambhogakaya*; it is the world of the origin's body and mind which existed from the beginning. He who has been absolved of all his sins and karma will have nothing remaining in his mind. When his self that is a sinner dies and disappears, God's world becomes his mind. His self and the world that is reborn as the true Soul and Spirit in God's world will live eternally without death.

Once you have been absolved of all your sins and karma and neither your self nor your mind world remains, you can go to the origin, the land of God and the Creator. The land you go to after the death of your false self is the land of God. Man lives in a world with innumerable worries, thoughts and delusions, with countless sufferings and burden but the land of God is one of freedom and liberation where there is no birth, old age, sickness or death; a world that is free from everything. This world is Truth, a complete world.

According to the Korean book of prophecy *Gyok-am-yu-rok*, one should not seek the ten havens of earth but he should seek the havens of the sky. The havens of the sky is heaven, a land of completeness itself where you just live, having laid down all burden; a land that is eternally alive.

During a talk with a clergyman, I spoke about people who try to go to heaven without repenting their sins and cleansing their karma. This is comparable to trying to eat a chicken without plucking its feathers. With a laugh, I said that people try to go to heaven, the land of God with the cold and calculating mind of a snake. However just as a chicken cannot be eaten without first having plucked its feathers, one cannot go to heaven, the land of God, without having repented one's sin and karma. That is, one cannot achieve a result without first having gone through the process to achieve it.

Man may try to get to heaven without cleansing his sins and karma, but he will fail because there is no other way. Cleansing one's sin and karma is the way to the land of God; and only when there is a method to do so, can one actually get there. When this method comes out in the world, it is the way to achieving human completion, namely, becoming God.

This has become possible in Maum Meditation because Maum Meditation has the method to discard one's worst enemy - his own self. In Buddhism, *mahayana mahaparinirvana* means a "big" death: the complete elimination of one's false body and mind. *Parinirvana* refers to a complete death without any remains. This is the way to get to the land of God. Christ's death on the cross teaches us that death is the bridge between man and God.

The world after the death of one's false self is the land of God; a forever-living, never-dying world; a world of freedom; a world of happiness itself. He who dies and is born in God's world while he is living is God.

Ideal Literature And The Ideal World

We think of the ideal as something that cannot possibly be realized - a hollow idea. However, the ideal is to achieve the state of completion, which is the ultimate goal of man, and such is its true meaning.

Ideal literature can guide man to the level of completion, and one that has an accompanying method and plan.

Because man is incomplete, he has tried to become complete through religion and other forms of meditation, but it was never achieved because until now, the method to do so did not exist.

Since man has a world of his own mind in which he lives, only when this world is destroyed and he becomes one with the mind of the world, the world of the origin, can the human race become one and man become complete. Only then can his Soul and Spirit become an eternally-living, never-dying immortal.

When we return to the mind of the origin, everyone will have the mind of wisdom, the mind of oneness. The human race will be able to live in peace forever.

Man thinks that only what is in his mind and is his, is right; however the mind of man is the mind of pictures taken of the world and is not reality; it is false and untrue. There is nothing right within it.

The ideal literature will have the method and plan for what man has been aiming to achieve - the education of the whole person - and when this happens, the ideal world will begin.

The ideal world is a complete world where people are not discontented with reality. It is a world that lacks for nothing, free from all the preconceptions and habits of the human world. Only when one returns to the mind of the origin, can man's mind shed all suffering and can he become a person of true freedom. Then he will live for others because he will not lack anything.

Through this book, this literature, countless people all over the world have discarded their false selves. Through the method to become a complete person, they are becoming complete. Therefore this book is not delusion, illusion or fiction but ideal literature that can be fulfilled in reality.

Until now, the human race was incomplete because the method to discard one's self and mind world and return to the origin did not exist. Now that it does exist, the human race will become complete.

Through ideal literature, the ideal world will be realized. Falseness will become Truth, and man's false mind will be changed to the real mind of God when he discards his self and his mind world. When man becomes the real mind of the origin, God's mind, he will always be happy, for he will no longer lack for anything, and be free from suffering and agonies.

If literature does not contain a method to discard his self, it is simply the stuff of daydreams and delusions; but if it does, it is ideal literature that can be realized.

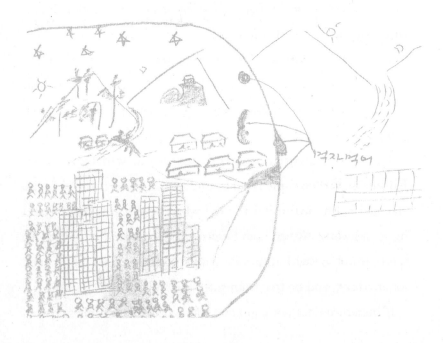

The Era Of Being Educated To Become Complete People

The South Korean Ministry of Education has often spoken of educating the whole person. In schools, a "whole person" has often been termed *ji deok che ye* (understanding, virtue, health and courtesy) and there has been much discussion on this topic. In China, the whole person is called *ji in yong* (understanding, benevolence, courage) and this is what is meant by *ji deok che ye* in Korean.

The real meaning of a "whole person" is a person who is complete. A complete person is a true person whose true soul never dies. Such a person is called a saint. Man will live a life of righteousness when this term is no longer just empty words and jargon and he actually becomes a true person and lives as one. While man has craved and struggled to become complete, it has not been easy because he is incomplete and false. Completion means one must be alive, without death.

In order for man to become righteous, we must first know about the set-up of the human mind. A human-being is a camera that takes pictures of what belongs to the world. Even though man thinks that he lives in the world, the moment he sees the world he takes a picture of it in his mind and lives inside the picture that he has taken. This is why man is false. The world and the human mind are overlapping so man mistakenly thinks that he is living in the world.

Isn't everything he experienced within his mind? What he has seen with the eyes, heard with the ears, smelled with the nose, tasted with the mouth, every word spoken and everything felt is all engraved within his mind. The human mind is like a photocopier that makes copies of what belongs to the world and all that happens in the world. The human mind is a copier that makes copies of the world. Even though man believes he lives in the world, he does not live in the world and because he is living in his own mind world he is unable to become a complete person.

In order to become a complete person, a whole person, one must start subtracting from his mind, to which, until now, he has always added. Only then can he walk the path to human completion. Truth is revealed to the extent the pictures, which are false, have been discarded. Completion is when a man who is false becomes true. Until now people have always added more and more in their lives. However when one subtracts the pictures inside his false mind world and discards his self that is living in that false world, he can become complete and recover his original nature.

The term "original nature" means simply, the nature of the origin. The nature of the origin is God's mind, the mind of Truth. If the copied human mind is gone, one can find his original nature. What originally existed before being copied is the original nature, the world. The reason you can exist in the world is the earth, the ground, exists. The earth exists because the sky which is the original foundation exists. Becoming the mind of this sky is to regain your original nature. If man's false mind and his self dies completely and only this mind of the sky, which is Truth remains, then man can regain his original nature.

When one is born again in this original nature which is the sky, he is born in the righteous land which is Truth. Therefore, he has no death and is the world itself. He will know all the ways of the world and become a person of wisdom itself. He will live a life of nature's flow. The world will then become a paradise on Earth with no thieves or bad people.

Currently, education focuses on the knowledge and skills needed to make a living. If one first becomes a whole person, a complete person, he will know all the ways of the world; consequently he will be even better at his studies and live a better life.

It is now the time of recovering one's original nature. In these times, the country where people first regain their original nature first will be one where people live better lives. Maum Meditation is the place where you can recover your original nature and since it is the place where it can actually be achieved, many people have come and many of them have already regained their original nature.

What Had To Come Has Finally Come

I travel all over the world, again and again, to hold seminars. The content of the talks I give at the seminars is the following: Man has copied the world and all that has happened to him in the world; he lives in a false world of his own mind; and he must escape from this fake picture world into the true world because without being resurrected in the true world, he cannot live eternally.

Most people seem to understand when they are told that they can become the saints they have only heard about if they cleanse all of their sins and karma and are reborn as Truth. I tell people that it is now the age when anyone can go to heaven and furthermore, it is nonsense to claim to be able to go to heaven without first becoming true while one is living. Heaven is a place where only Truth, God lives. Therefore if one does not become Truth he will die forever because he is false.

I say that Truth is an existence that never changes and lives eternally; and that the land of Truth is a world beyond the complete death of one's self.

I also ask them to imagine that they had not been born in the world. They nod when I say to them that the Universe would still exist even if they had not been born. Then I ask them to imagine that all material matter in the Universe had not been created. When I ask them whether the empty sky still exists, they again all nod. I tell them that this empty sky is the Creator, God, Buddha and Allah.

A person who dies after living eighty years in the world disappears - he no longer exists. Everyone agrees when I tell them that the empty sky, which is the origin, the source and Truth existed an eternity ago, exists even now and from the perspective of the empty sky, man lives a life comparable to a split second then vanishes.

Doesn't the empty sky simply just exist, regardless of whether man exists? Hasn't everything in the world from ten million years ago, i.e. the trees, rabbits, deer, lions and people, all disappeared? It is the way of the world and Truth that everything in the heavens and earth comes from the origin, the original foundation, and returns to it.

I tell them that only he who discards his false human mind, changes to the real mind of God, and is reborn in the land of God while he is living can live forever. I tell them that they must become the mind of the empty sky - the mind of God and Buddha - and in the land born of this substance, they must also be reborn as this substance in order to live as an eternal never-dying immortal.

In the world only the existence of the empty sky is eternal, and in the land of this existence a place of eternity does not exist without being reborn as its substance. One's vague notions of heaven are just his own delusions.

The conclusion is that one must change his false mind into the real mind and be reborn in the world of the real mind. It is discarding one's false self so that his real self may be born. When people hear this, they often compare it to what they have learned through their religion. However there were many who said that if there is such a method, that they were willing to try and started meditating.

There was a person who failed to become Truth despite trying various religions as well as many other things. Despite his efforts, he felt unable to love his enemies, and had the same likes and dislikes as he had always had. However, he realized that his self was false. When he attended the seminar and listened to the talk given, he exclaimed, "What had to come has finally come!" and began meditating. He was eventually born in the land of Truth. Sometime later when I met him again, I asked him if he felt able to love his enemies and whether he still had likes and dislikes. He replied that he felt able to love his enemies and he no longer had likes and dislikes. When I asked him further whether he has achieved everything and become Truth he replied that he has achieved everything and has indeed, become Truth.

A Plan For The Human Race

Korean politicians have been fighting incessantly for a long time. Their actions arouse worry and unrest, when instead they should be uniting to come up with a plan for the betterment of the country's citizens. Each politician boasts of his own merits with slick words and insists that only his own opinion is correct - it is truly funny to watch. In this tiny country, every province has its own political party. This regionalism is divisive and not conducive to national harmony.

No plan exists to cooperate and work together even in this state of affairs. Even if there was a plan it would not be executed. Of the systems of government man has made, communism has crumbled and capitalism has reached its limit. It would be best for people to repent and realize their wrong-doings; know that everything is their own fault; subtract the false bubble that is their selves and live as true people.

Man would find life in the world easier if he knew and accepted the ways of the world. Instead, he tries to change the world to suit him but this is impossible. Consequently he finds life in the world difficult, for his mind is opposite to the ways of the world.

Only when man recovers his true self, the origin, will he live with the mind that has become one with the world, the mind of the origin. At such a time, he will have wisdom and only then will there be a proper plan for human life. While one might think in his mind that his thoughts and will are correct, there is nothing that is righteous in man; thus there can be no proper plan.

Once one sees from the viewpoint of the world, coming up with such a plan is very easy. When everyone in the human race discards his individual wrongful notions, habits and consciousness, and changes to the mind of the world, everyone will become of one mind and every thought and action will be right. A proper plan will then emerge because everyone's mind will be one.

We waste a vast amount of time being educated but many people still live in hardship because what should be the basics and foundation of all education is missing; namely, how to find the right mind and live a righteous life. Thus people do not have wisdom within the knowledge they have acquired. If one has a righteous mind, his actions and life will accordingly be righteous also. As he will have a rightful way of thinking, he will no longer insist that his own party's opinions and plans are correct when they are not, and he will be able to acknowledge what is right even when it is not his own.

Man does not know what is right or what is proper because of the self-centered mind he has. When he throws this away and becomes the mind of the world, he will have a righteous mind.

Part 4

The Everlasting World

Man lives inside his mind of delusion,

but when he changes his human mind

to the mind of the sky before the sky that is eternally alive,

he is able to truly live.

The Human Mind II

The flowing river has flowed past;

silently, it flowed somewhere.

It was not within the sounds made when it collided with
    various things;

and though it made its way by winding here and there,

it was not within the mind of those paths.

Always flowing downward according to the universal order
    of nature,

water that flows silently,

does not possess knowledge,

or any kinds of minds whatsoever.

It may seem as though the many things in the world

have their own numerous events and stories,

but this perception is just a manifestation of the human mind.

All things just live.

Only inside the human mind,

do countless different minds exist.

The World Beyond Time

Cloud, please stay -

Wind, please blow -

Do not dwell within time, following its passage,

but live beyond it, outside of time.

The flowing river has gone with time,

the flowing years have also gone with time,

the countless things in existence and non-existence,

including the many stories of life,

have all gone with the passage of time.

Everything that lives bound to time is consumed by it -

the devil that consumes everything.

So do not be consumed by time,

nor blame it.

Only the world that is beyond time

is the complete world,

where meaningless life stories have all disappeared.

The Mind Of Nature

The sky is so clear,
it is a shade of blue
that appears almost black.
Flowing in the valley between the mountains,
the water in the stone-bedded stream is inexpressibly clear,
and in it, nameless fish dart here and there, playing.

The mountains are high,
and here and there flowers are in bloom.
New leaves are budding on treetops,
in the mountains, wild herbs are sprouting,
and many fresh shoots can be seen on the hardy kiwi trees.
Following the mountain valley,
I stumble on a patch of wild mountain vegetables.
As I forage for mountain herbs
seeking out spots yet untouched by people,
the warm sun, the clear air and water
refreshes my body, worn and stained by the city.
My body feels as light as a feather.
Taking after the surroundings, my whole body feels so clean,
and thanks to all the hiking I did in my youth,

I do not tire despite walking up many hills.

I sit on a large rock near the water to eat my packed lunch.
There is a small waterfall close by
and on a slope near the cascade, a bird I cannot identify
quietly chatters as it flits back and forth.

In spring, there are so many things in the mountainside
too beautiful to enjoy alone;
the day is warm,
and I begin to wonder how long it has been
since someone last came by the places I have been.
These high mountains and secluded valleys are hard to get to,
and I wonder whether anyone has ever been here.

Climbing higher up the mountain,
I can see there are less leaves growing on the trees,
and a startled mountain deer runs away,
casting back sidelong looks as it runs.
The animals and vegetation here in the mountains
live generation after generation, just like people.
Without homes, with only their naked selves,
facing the winds if the winds are blowing,
the rain if the rain is falling,
and the snow if it is snowing;

in the cold if it is cold,

and in the heat if it is hot,

they live without words.

Everything that exists disappears,

comes again, then again disappears.

But only I know the principle

that the place they returned to is the origin,

and it is the origin from whence they came.

Trying to seek and attain something from this transient world,

so many people fight, kill and thieve;

in my eyes, they are truly foolish.

One has become the mind of nature

when he is without the mind of blame,

without envy, jealousy or conceit,

without judgment of right and wrong,

discernment of this and that;

when all human minds have disappeared,

his mind is the mind of nature.

The Mind Before Human Minds

The countless things that silently come and silently leave,
come from great nature and return to great nature.
Man lives according to what is in his mind,
but the mind before his mind is the mind of great nature.
Regardless of whether things come and go,
great nature is silent.
And regardless of whether things go and come,
great nature exists, silently.
All forms that come and go, and go and come,
are incomplete.
Only he who has returned to the place of the origin
from whence all creation comes forth,
knows the providence of coming and going.
Even if all things in the world change,
the original world, which brought forth nature,
will not change.
Only this existence is Truth and only it is real.
People are dead because they do not have this mind of Truth
and they are not born in the world of this mind.
Living in his own mind world
and unable to become one with the true world that exists,

man is trapped within the mind he has

and thus ends up dying an eternal death.

He who knows he is the most pathetic, useless existence in the
world

and therefore detests himself, has the right to become Truth;

while he who greedily consumes and tries to possess
everything,

he whose self tries to accomplish Truth or become Truth,

is far from Truth.

Truth is the place before all creation;

Truth is the place before human form and human mind.

In order to become Truth, one's body and mind must not
exist -

only then can one go to the land of Truth,

and it is the master of the true land

who allows him to be reborn in this land.

Only when man stops seeking something

and completely denies his self

can he be reborn and live in the true kingdom.

If we are not born in heaven while living,

we will die eternally.

Unless your mind returns to the origin of the Universe

and is reborn from that origin,

the word *eternal* cannot and does not apply to you.

Only the place of the origin is eternal;

only this place is the forever-living and never-dying immortal;
and only in this place will you be reborn as the never dying
    immortal.
Truth is this place,
and only one reborn as Truth will live.

Enter Into The Season Of Truth

Following the passage of time
the world, the rivers, the mountains, and I, change.
Before fleeting human life existed,
the world existed,
as did the original world that brought forth the world.

The original world always just existed,
just as it is, without change,
from before the beginning and until an eternity afterward,
regardless of man's existence.
But man who lives within the years
passes away with the years.
From ancient times many spoke of life's transience -
that it is like a drifting cloud,
a floating weed;
that human life truly does not exist.
But no one knew what this meant.

Now that I have entered into the season of becoming Truth
I know that human life is futile;
that the life man lives simply passes away in this world.

Now that I have become Truth and I know Truth,

I know that what the elders said of human life is true -

man is unable to become one with the world;

he engraves the world in his mind

and inside that world, he lives as an illusion.

His life is just a picture.

Many people risk their lives to succeed

in this false and meaningless life,

but this is just their own minds.

It is when one's mind has become the mind of Truth

that he does not live in the false world but in the true world.

It was not possible to know Truth

because no one knew or had become Truth.

However, the time to enter into the season has now come:

To enter into the season is to become Truth,

and that time is now.

The World Of A False Dream

There is no way to know how many people have lived
in the long ages that have passed silently by.
Across the river where peach blossoms bloom,
a few tile-roofed houses
dot through a village of thatched cottages.
Idle children and housewives run out of each house,
to watch the stranger passing by.
There are other villages, here and there along the way,
and at the entrance to one village,
there is a rundown store.
I stop by and in a big clay jar
a gourd floats on an alcoholic brew.
In the barley fields, men-folk in traditional garments
are digging furrows; the lush green barley has grown
so it hangs over the furrows, hiding them.
In the sky, a lark is chirping,
and the people working in the fields alone
are without worries, accepting their work as their calling.
The walls of the alleyways distinguish each adobe house
and they feel familiar, even though it's my first time here.
Further along I come across a stream

with a bridge of stepping stones, and I carefully cross.

The spring air has started to melt the ice, clouding it as it
    thaws;

the water is cloudy yet so clear.

A frog floats on top of the water,

and a school of carp swims by.

Lush grass grows alongside the banks,

and the warm sun makes the shimmering heat rise.

I flop down on the ground

not wanting to walk further.

In each house people pay homage to their ancestors

up to the previous five generations,

and only they, the descendants, generation by generation,

are proof ancient people existed.

This is a place conquered, taken, then lost

during the time of the Three Kingdoms.

Where has the thunder of horses' hooves gone?

Where are the famous generals now?

Events of those ancient times flicker through my mind.

There is a mountain in the distance;

I have always wanted to climb it

but it is a difficult hike.

The strong scent of pine trees perfumes the mountain trail

and as I follow the path,

the hairs on the back of my head stand up

even though it is still the middle of the day.

They say a tiger lived on this mountain in the old days

and as I climb up bend after bend,

my breathing becomes labored,

and after a long while, I reach the peak.

I climb on a rock to a wide open view and look down,

and see a village in the distance.

Many would have climbed this mountain,

each with their different stories.

What would they have thought about as they climbed up?

I hurry down the mountain

and the stream becomes a waterfall;

its cascade is truly magnificent.

The current is strong,

and the sound of the water echoes as it flows down the valley.

Deep in the mountains, I come across a lone abandoned
      cottage.

It is hard to know when someone last lived here -

perhaps he left or passed away,

for the lonely thatched cottage is silent.

Walking down the long trail, I see a few more homes

then a small village appears.

The inhabitants are the descendants

of those who fled a war during the *Shilla* Dynasty.

Their adobe homes are falling apart

and they look so impoverished.
I travel on down the winding path and the valley grows larger.
As I pass by another village,
I see a few men leisurely hanging around a storefront
garbed in traditional attire and smoking bamboo pipes.
The village dog follows and barks at me, an unknown
   stranger -
I just walk on with no particular place in mind.

In the heavily populated urban cities I have visited,
everyone lives busy lives.
Those with jobs are buried by their work,
and those without work are idle, but worry about food and
   survival.
When I became Truth, I realized the world and all the people
   I met
were of the world of a false dream.
The people were ghosts and it was the world of ghosts;
although beautiful memories remain in my mind,
they are just pictures.
Now that I am out in the real world,
I know that life in the world was inside an illusion.
I had lived in my mind overlapping the world;
I had lived so foolishly.
It was all a false dream.

Futile Human Life

The human mind is one of hunger
that tries to fill itself
with even more minds of hunger.
It is a habit of this mind to want to be filled;
but no matter how a person with this mind tries,
it can never be filled;
this is the reason he suffers.
The world changes along with time that flies by
but everything that happened over the years remain in his
    mind,
these stories have become his self, driving him raving mad;
and he does not know that they are just illusions.
Such is the reason human life is in vain;
why it is the life of a non-existent illusion.

The Poem Of Youth That Has Passed

Silently, my youth disappeared

with the years that passed without a word,

and my body is different from the days of its youth.

My life was spent in futile busy activities,

but it became more and more meaningless.

Everything that I achieved and wanted to achieve

was in vain and empty.

It was a life in a time when man could not become complete

and it was the time of a dream,

in which I had resentments and grudges.

After waking from the dream, I found it such a relief,

that all I wanted to have and achieve were not fulfilled.

In the dream, without once waking,

I lived wandering and wandering the dream world

without a day's rest from my scripted dream.

If there are any regrets about the years that have passed,

it is that I did not wake sooner from the dream

to do the work of the awakened world.

It was only when I awoke from the dream

that I was able to know everything in the dream

were all false things and falsely done.

The law of the world is that all material things in existence
disappear with the years; this is nature's law, Truth,
but I was only able to know this when I woke from the dream.
All desires and bitterness exist inside the dream.
While I was in the dream
I was filled with bitterness and I had many desires
but it is a relief among reliefs,
that I was not able to fulfill those desires
or resolve my bitterness.
Perhaps that is why I easily awoke from the dream.

Who is the great man and who is the fool?
Only in the dream are there great men and fools.
Outside the dream, everybody is one and lives in freedom.
I have no regrets for my youth that has gone;
I will do what I have to do
without complaining that the time remaining is too short
and then silently leave this body behind,
but in the world I worked for -
the world of the Soul and Spirit -
many people will be saved and my land will prosper;
and I will be waiting,
for the people who will live eternally with me.

A Mountain Hike In Winter

White snow blankets the mountains and streams everywhere.

Hikers who enjoy snow-scapes

are climbing up a path piled knee-deep in snow.

I cannot see the path, but following their footprints,

I climb higher and higher.

My whole body sweats, and it trickles down my forehead.

After the snowfall a cold wind blows, scattering the fallen
    snow;

piled atop the branches it looks like lovely snow flowers.

Bend after bend, we wind up and up,

and after hours of panting and puffing

my whole body is wringing wet with perspiration

and my drenched underwear feels cold.

Near the summit, the trees are no longer tall

but short and scrawny, with snow-blossoms on their branches.

The sight is truly magnificent.

The summit looks close, and I climb towards it

with all my strength.

Many are already there calling out, "Hooray!"

expressing the joy of having reached the top to their heart's content.

Everyone is happy and relaxed.

Even though it is cold and the temperature is below freezing,

people are gathered in groups here and there,

basking in the happiness that only those

who have hiked to the top of this mountain can feel -

no one else can know the feeling of this moment.

It is so cold that some drink a shot of *soju*;

some students have already had a shot or two on the way up.

One among them has become so drunk,

his eyes are bleary and his legs have given way.

The other students cannot carry him down

so I, and several others, take turns and carry him on our backs

and climb down the slippery, rugged mountain.

I put him down at a mountain temple

and tell them to give him some sugar water.

As I turn to leave silently, they ask for my address,

but I tell them it is ok, and slip quietly away.

It is a big mountain;

even after many bends

I am still in the mountain valley.

Only those who have been here

would know how my whole body feels.

In the gorges and valleys

there are cottages scattered sparsely.

They are old, worn, and look so shabby.

It seems the tenant farmers who cultivate the terraced fields

have difficulty making ends meet,

for the clothes they wear in the cold weather are worn and tattered;

they look so poor.

The stream flows on under the ice.

After a long walk down, I reach the parking lot.

I drop by the tavern and order a bowl of *makgeolli*

and some fish-cake soup;

I doubt there is anyone who knows how good they taste!

I do not get drunk, even though I drink more than usual,

I just feel good, perhaps because my body feels good.

Pleasantly tipsy, I head home.

As I gaze upon the falling snow here in New York

and the snow flowering on the branches,

those days when I freely hiked up and down mountains

have turned into longing - I do not know

if I will ever be able to hike here and there as I used to.

With the thought that I may never have those moments again,

whether it be because of old age or lack of time,

my longing grows.

Man Would Not Know Even If Truth Came Or Left

A cloud lingers.

Many clouds have come and gone in the empty sky

but now, there is not a single trace of them.

I show people the origin of Truth, but they are unable to see.

They cannot see,

because there is no Truth within the human mind.

In the many ages that have passed by,

countless people have tried to achieve Truth

without knowing its meaning and purpose - what Truth is.

Innumerable traces of their efforts remain,

but no *dō-in*, a person of Truth, has ever existed

because man tried to find and achieve Truth with himself,

not knowing Truth means one is born in the land of Truth

by discarding his self so that only Truth remains.

If someone had achieved Truth,

there would already be a method to become Truth.

While many people sacrificed their precious youth seeking
   Truth

their frustrated sighs were the only result,

and after a lifetime of years wasted,

they died of old age or sickness.

Time has taken their regrets and their lives.

The years continue to pass,

and no one knows where they have gone.

Later after many years, people drew their own delusional
     images of Truth

so that to each would have been his own thoughts.

In the past, a hero was a person who killed many people

while a saint was a person who talked about Truth

and prophesied its coming as a human-being.

Truth must come as a person

in order for people to become Truth.

For people to become complete,

a completed person must come.

All the scriptures told of this happening some day

but not a single person knows when that day will be

nor would anyone know even if it had already arrived

because there is no Truth in man's mind.

All that exists inside man's mind

are the preconceptions and habits from the pictures he has
     taken,

and bound by those self-centered conceptions and behaviors

he cannot know the true will of Truth.

People would not know even if the Savior comes or leaves.
Only those who become Truth will know.

Let's Go To The Living World

The world is alive,

but man is not.

The world simply just exists,

but man has countless hardships and dreams unreal dreams -

he does not know it is all meaningless and false

for he is not Truth,

and he dies after a lifetime of agony and anguish.

He is urgently told that one lives forever,

but he does not realize the true meaning of these words.

Isn't it natural and logical that one dies

if he has not become Truth?

Man thinks that someone will save him even if he has not

become Truth

but this idea is wrong;

so come to your senses and strive to become Truth,

for becoming Truth is of the utmost importance.

The world and man is what is real and false:

the world is real and man is false.

It is nonsense to think that one can live eternally

when his mind has not become the eternal world

and he has not been born in that land.

Do not try to find or achieve something,

for Truth is revealed only when one discards his false self

and the only thing man must do is to be born,

in the land of Truth by the will of Truth's master.

If this is not done there is no purpose or reason for living.

Instead of living a human life of seventy or eighty years

live an eternal life, live to the life of the world -

only such a person is wise.

He who tries to possess more, commits more sins

while he who discards and eliminates even his self

can be born into the world of Truth.

One whose mind has become Truth has heaven in his mind;

the whole world lives

and he himself is born in his mind.

If there is only the mind of God within you

and no human minds at all,

you no longer take pictures and the master of the Soul and
    Spirit exists within you.

Your true soul must be born in the land of that original
    foundation

if you are to become a forever-living immortal.

He who talks of going to heaven after death

when he has not gone to heaven while he is living

cannot go to heaven; he dies forever.

The Reason No One In The World Sees Truth

When the day is clear,

you can see the sky clearly.

When your mind is clear and clean

you can see the sky clearly.

Everything is one, and everything is Truth

but there is no one in the world who sees Truth

for man is not born in the world,

and he is living in his own world made of pictures.

It is a world of his mind;

a world of illusions;

a world of feces;

a world of ghosts;

it is not the real world; it is a picture.

Everyone is dead, without exception,

with everything trapped inside their minds.

Being born in the true world means

destroying the world of pictures - one's mind world -

so as to be truly born in the world.

Even When They Are Told That The Place Of Truth Is Where One Becomes True, They Cannot Hear

Time is passing by and I am getting older.

Silent, fleeting time is the devil that gobbles up everything in
the world.

Everyone lives life without knowing its meaning and purpose,

then succumbs to the devil of time,

ignorant of where he is headed.

Man wants to live awhile longer and cannot let go;

he leaves behind his regrets, tears, his last will and testament,

then departs this world, this human life.

People do not know where the dead have gone

and because they themselves have never died

they do not know the world beyond death.

It is only possible to know that world after one has experienced
death.

The world man goes to after death is a false world

that does not exist in the land of Truth.

He passes away after living his one human life -

and he is dead forever.

He is dead because his Soul and Spirit is not born in the
kingdom of Truth.

The people of old blamed life, calling it meaningless and in
    vain.
Did they blame it because the life they lived disappeared,
or because they do not exist in the world?
I want to ask them,
but they have all passed away so there is no way to know.
Human life disappears like a dream, a cloud, or smoke,
leaving behind so much resentment and bitterness
in so many stories that could not be told.
Man lives life building and building his castle,
living only for himself, as if he will live forever.
But he accomplishes nothing and has nothing -
his life is like a floating cloud.
No one has the wisdom to know this,
so man lives bound by his own chains.
All the things that come and go, appear and disappear,
but everyone lives one life and then disappears
in ignorance of where one comes from and returns to.
The true compassion and love of heaven has not forsaken us;
it has without fail given us this time, this thankful season,
of saving our pitiful lives and the world in existence.
Without fail this time has come,
but man, bound by his own chains, does not know the time he
    is in.
Inside his burden, man who has hunger

does not know the world, the events of the world,

nor the true will of the world.

He cannot hear the call to live a lifetime of the world,

instead of living a lifetime of a meaningless human life.

When one seeks from within useless scraps,

from within the burden he carries,

all that he finds will be useless scraps.

In that place, with that mind, all one does

is speak the words of one mentally unsound;

the words of a ghost, a delusion.

One might babble the events of the true world,

or stories of the true world stolen from the books he has read,

but he who devours all things just consumes what is false.

He does not understand that Truth is in the place where one
   becomes true,

and continues to devour false scraps.

If the place you are attending is Truth

shouldn't you already be Truth yourself?

Isn't the only place that is real and true,

the place where one actually becomes true and real?

If you have ears, then hear these words,

and if you feel these words are right, applaud;

then seek out the place where one can become true,

become Truth, and be born as a righteous person in the land of
   righteousness.

We need to come to our senses;

we must know what we should seek and do.

Whether time or the rivers or all that is the world's passes by,

he who greets the everlasting world

is a person who is wise and blessed.

The Original Birthplace

Do you know your original birthplace?
It is not where you were physically born;
it is the original foundation that is the source and the origin -
a place of great freedom without obstacles or hindrances.

Those who have left their original birthplace
do not want to return because of their sins;
they have acquired many illusions while living away from
    home,
and it is in those illusions that they now live.
They have forgotten their birthplace;
they do not even bother to think about such things.
In the original birthplace the parents' hearts must bleed
when they think of their suffering children.
They are asking their children to return instead of suffering far
    from home,
that they will give them the world of the birthplace and
    cleanse away their sins,
so that they may live with a clean mind and body.
Believing the sins to be interesting and fun,
the children live in sin, not knowing they are in sin.

Can there be anything more pitiful and frustrating?

Don't live by yourself far from home only to die and disappear.

Come back to your birthplace,

cleanse away your sins and become a new person;

become an eternal and never-dying immortal,

and live forever in your birthplace with your parents.

Then, there are no worries, no anxieties, and no stress;

the five desires and seven sins and *tamjinchi* -

desires, anger, foolishness - do not exist;

it is the state of freedom and liberation,

free from all human suffering and all human conceptions and
    habits.

It is a place beyond everything of the human world.

Let's live forever with peace of mind and freedom,

in this place.

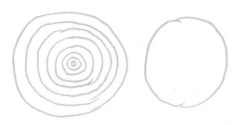

My Will

Deep in the night,

a nameless bird sings sadly from a tree.

Long ago, when I was studying

in a mountain temple, steeped in solitude,

the hoots of an owl and the gurgle of a flowing stream

would sound throughout the night.

Those lonely times of solitude have changed to longing.

There was a time when countless thoughts boiled over in my
     head;

a time when I was chased by my circumstances

but did not achieve anything.

Now with hindsight, I see it is fortunate

I did not fulfill any of my big ideals.

I was not a great person,

and I lived ridiculing myself;

disliking, ignoring and cursing myself;

telling myself that I was the one who was wrong.

Perhaps this is why I did not have much to repent.

I was not great in any way

so I was humble and I worked hard.

As a result, I lived well

compared to the days of scarcity in my childhood.
Of the years that silently passed, during the time
when I first started teaching Truth in Mount Gaya,
I again heard the cries of that owl every night;
the owl that had struck a chord in my lonely heart.

Everyone who sought me out each came to me
with fifty thousand thoughts.
As they shed these fifty thousand agonies,
they showed the forms of their minds
in fifty thousand different ways.
Only then did I realize man is uglier, dirtier,
and infinitely more vile than I was.
When I had scolded myself,
telling myself that I was dirty, ugly,
and the worst person in the world,
it had been an unknowing repentance.

With the title of *dō-in*, I awaken people.
I cannot describe the joy I felt
when after many nights meditating together till dawn,
those countless people, who had laughed and cried
within their fifty thousand agonies, enlightened to the Truth.
I had also felt happy when I escaped from the grave
and came out into the world,

but I had more joy in their enlightenment than I had in my
    own,
which was boundless each time a person's consciousness
changed from falseness to Truth.
It was the first time in the world
people were truly becoming enlightened,
and as the founder,
the fact that people were actually achieving Truth
was tremendously moving.
People's fifty thousand agonies decreased
as they moved up through the levels,
but there were those who tried to achieve Truth
inside the framework of their selves,
which is something man grimly holds onto until the end.
Those whose false selves tried to enlighten to the Truth,
were unable to ignore their false selves or progress further
and ultimately did not achieve Truth.
However those who were like bears and did not give up,
those who were constant and had thankful hearts
are still meditating and are close to completion.
Time flew by silently,
and since then twelve, thirteen years have passed.
I started teaching Truth in my mid-forties,
but now my hair has turned grey
and my youth and energy have vanished.

I am entering into old age;

I am becoming a wrinkled grandpa,

with grey hair and ground-down teeth.

My body does not move as I will it to, as it did in my youth.

The world is wide,

but I am living a human life with only seventy to eighty years,

and there is so much left to do in the world.

So regardless of whether it is day or night,

all my time is dedicated to teaching people Truth.

My mind is busy, so busy, with the constant thought

that people all over the world must be awakened;

and I am waiting and waiting,

for the day when all people have become complete,

and all people are able to live.

It is my hope that before I die,

Truth will be spread all over the world

and everyone will be resurrected as Truth.

I pity people who live and die without meaning or purpose;

it is heartbreaking.

It is my will to work hard

so that even one more person may live.

The Alcohol I Drank In The Past World

Above the tavern without a street number,

the sky is clear, without a cloud to be seen.

It is a warm, spring day,

and the tavern sits alone

on a road set apart from the village.

It is a place where village people stop for a drink,

as well as those coming and going from the market.

There is an old barmaid,

who has been making her living here for a long time.

Weary from walking, I stop and order a kettle of *makgeolli*.

With *kimchi* on the side, I pour glass after glass and drink.

Farmers on their break order huge bowls of *makgeolli*,

and they gulp it down with some salt

and hurry straight back to work.

Clear water flows in the creek out front,

and the village womenfolk and girls who came to do the
    laundry

sweep sideways glances at me.

They lay the clothes down on the stepping-stones

and beat it with their laundry paddles.

One glass, two glasses, three, four, five,

six glasses later, the whole kettle is gone.

In the yard, a hen clucks,

leading her brood of yellow chicks around.

Seeing as the village is quite large,

I suppose many would have visited the tavern with their stories
   and events.

There will be some who laughed and cried;

some who had regrets in their hearts,

and some who drank joyfully.

There would have been some who wanted to end it all

but after a drink, let it go, and did not go through with it.

The tavern is old and worn,

but I feel an inexplicable affection for it,

and I find myself ordering and drinking another kettleful.

The old barmaid at least, has smoothly oiled back her hair

and is tidily attired.

This barmaid granny asks me,

Young man, who are you and where do you come from?

She nods while I explain where I live

and why I am traveling on this road by the tavern.

After I empty two kettles, I pay the bill and set off.

The day is hazy from the heat waves

and I can hear the sound of water trickling along the creek.

Lush green grass is growing everywhere

and there are fish swimming in the water.

After walking silently for awhile,

I subconsciously burst into song.

I alone am merry,

singing under the influence of the wine,

and a farmer pauses his work to watch me.

I reach my destination just as I sober up.

I meet my friend, and we go to another tavern

where we drink more wine.

The wine splashes raucously into the bottom of the glass.

I can feel it spreading all through my body;

I become tipsy, my tongue trips and slurs,

and the discontent inside me begins to boil,

and I curse for no particular reason -

damn people and damn the world!

As we drink, my friend and I blame the world

that does not bend to our will.

We finally head to my friend's house to sleep as the day begins
    to dawn.

I have to be half carried and dragged because I have been
    drinking all day.

I lie down in my friend's room and fall asleep immediately.

My friend likes to drink as much as I do, so the next day,

we go to chase our hangovers with another drink.

Going from bar to bar, we drink,

then we drink some more.

Without meaning or purpose, another day passes
with the sounds of our voices calling,
Pour! and, *drink*!
The day after, I finally leave my friend's house,
and make my way home.

In my youth, I could not achieve what I wanted.
I wasted many days with alcohol,
and the affairs of the world were not to my liking.
Why people live, who goes to hell
and who goes to heaven after they die -
these questions always battled inside me
and I think I already knew the futility of life.
Time passed in various ways,
then when I was almost sixty,
I traveled by car back to that road.
The tavern was gone, the barmaid granny had passed away
and when I visited my friend's house,
it was his son that came out to greet me.
He told me his father had become ill and died.
Even though I had been busy and rarely heard news of him,
I still missed my affectionate friend.
The friend who had always smiled and listened
when I was annoyed or irritated has passed away,
and the people I knew in the past

have all scattered and gone on to the next world.

Just as it has always been said,

the life we live is really a dream.

Even the mountains and streams in my mind,

that I had seen then, are different now,

changed by the passing of time.

Now that I have come out into the true world

after living in the human world,

I find I had conversed with people that did not exist;

I had exchanged affections with people that did not exist;

I had laughed and cried inside a dream world;

a futile world;

an illusionary world;

a world that does not, does not exist.

I had lived inside a world of illusion,

made from pictures taken of the world.

Now that I live in the world that exists,

those memories no longer exist

and the place where I am is heaven and paradise.

Now that I have the mind of the world,

I no longer take pictures of the world or its affairs,

and it is freedom and liberation.

Now as I look back,

I am thankful for this self that was dissatisfied with the world,

and for not being able to accomplish my will or realize my

ideals.

I tore down and killed this self in my mind,

this self that cursed the world,

this self that blamed the world;

I ceaselessly killed and killed, and eliminated this self

until I became one with the mind of the world.

Now I know it was the false things inside my mind that

    tormented me,

my delusions that persecuted me,

my greed from my sense of inferiority that plagued me.

The silently passing time no longer exists,

and the memories of long ago was the world of hell.

It is immeasurably peaceful to live with the mind of the world;

my enemy had not been anybody else but myself.

I tore down my mind world and the foe that is my self;

I triumphed over myself.

Now I am reborn in the world with the mind of the world,

I am able to live to the age of the world.

Old Memories

The blizzard's blistering wind makes it difficult to see the way.
The times are good here in New York, where I am,
but I find myself longing for old memories.
Those old memories remind me of a time
when my ancestors of long ago roamed the steppes of
    Manchuria.
They all would have lived
following their lives,
following their thoughts,
following their greed.

Spring In New York

Everywhere, countless varieties of spring flowers are in bloom.

Nowhere in the world,

is there a more beautiful scene than this:

By every house, in every street,

in trees and garden beds, the flowers in bloom

are so, so beautiful.

Here is beautiful heaven,

heaven itself.

Many European immigrants came to live here in New York.

Now, there are no traces of the Indians from long ago,

instead most are Westerners and some Africans,

and only a few Asians.

The first generation immigrants,

and the people who are here from all over the world,

must miss their home country.

The first Europeans to arrive must have felt the same way -

as the second generation is born,

their homelands fade from memory

and exist only in their minds;

The homelands in their minds would no longer be there,

even if they went back.

Yet, they labor and labor to make a living in a foreign land

holding onto those memories of the past.

The rows of houses built a century ago make me think

America must have been a good place to live.

In the midst of this transitory place, there are those who stayed

but for an Asian such as myself,

it is hard to understand what they live for,

and what joy they find in living.

They live according to their customs,

yet adapting to the life here - a busy life.

This country is a capitalist society,

where money is held in the highest,

and it has dominated the world for a hundred years.

Now it is struggling in a financial crisis;

unemployment has risen,

people are not as caring as they once were,

and those who do not have jobs find life hard.

Even though I have been all over the world,

I find everyone thinks only about eating and living well;

without money, there is nowhere in the world you can live in
   peace.

There is nowhere I particularly want to live.

Communism has crumbled,

and even capitalism seems to have come as far as it can go.

The time of a spiritual civilization -

when all minds become one and everyone lives in comfort -

seems to have come.

A world will come,

a world with peace of mind

where anyone can work hard and live joyously.

When man discards his greed

and knows how to live within his means,

in such a world he will be able to live a better life.

When everyone becomes of one mind,

and the world becomes a place where people live for others,

it will become a paradise on Earth.

Heaven is this world,

and for a person who has been born in this true world,

this world is heaven.

This world and that world are not different but one.

One's true actions will remain in this world; as much as he
    does,

exactly that much, will remain in the living world.

As man gains more wisdom, and escapes from the world of his
    own mind,

this world will become one in which everyone can live well;

the whole world will be one's own wherever he goes,

and he will be able to live with comfort and peace.

The Age Of A New Heaven And A New Earth

The clouds have gone.

The winds have gone.

My delusions have gone.

I too have disappeared.

Everything in the Universe has all gone,

and the only thing that remains

is the place of consciousness

that exists amidst the nothingness.

Many pointless years were spent in busy activity and worries

because I was lost in my own delusions,

only to find in the end that though I was busy

I had nowhere to go.

With the silent passage of the years,

countless stories have all faded from memory

and yet those stories became me -

the false delusional being I call my self -

formed by my beliefs and habits.

My false mind, deeply rooted inside my heart

became my master, and I became the slave of illusions.

When I realized all my years living with those beliefs and
      habits,

those illusions, were all just pictures, I erased them.
Once I realized that even my existence was a picture
living in an illusion, I abandoned it.
Furthermore, I also eradicated the world inside my mind
so that only my true mind remained.

The true mind -
which does not disappear even when eliminated -
is Truth, the Creator, God and Buddha.
When the master of this existence comes as a human-being
he will guide people to the land of this existence,
and also enable people to be reborn as the *Jung* and *Shin* -
the body and mind - of this existence.
Since being born in the land of *Jung* and *Shin*,
which is life itself, I have gained new life.
Now after having discarded and eliminated the countless
    things
that had happened in the meaningless world,
only this true world remains.
Because I am reborn in the land of life,
the land of the true mind within me,
I will not die; I am immortal.
Just as so many prophets have foretold,
I have been reborn, resurrected,
and I have gone to eternal heaven while living.

The whole Universe has been created anew inside me
and in this land without death, I live forever and ever.
When you are born in the land of life within you,
when there is life within you,
it is you, yourself, that know this;
it is you, yourself, that knows you shall never die.

The flowing river exists because I exist.
Even if it flows, it is simply what it is: Truth.
That is to say, everything is Truth itself,
the original foundation.

It seems no less than a miracle
that the countless stories chattering and cluttering my mind
    have all gone,
and I write this poem born in the true land inside me.
Isn't this the beginning of a new heaven and a new earth?

The beginning of a new heaven and a new earth
is when heaven and the earth have completely disappeared
and a new heaven and a new earth is reborn in the true land.
It is resurrection in the land of *Jung* and *Shin*
as the true body and mind.
I have become that which I had never even dreamed,
that of whom we have only been told -

Buddha, a saint, a holy person -

only to find that all people in the world are dead;

I need to breathe life into them and save them.

Do not stake everything on the futile matters of life.

If we are all to go to the land of Truth

we need to cleanse our minds and get to the place of Truth,

the place where there is absolutely no self,

for he who is born in that land will live forever without death.

He who does not accomplish this during these blessed times

    will die forever,

while the one who lives, will live eternally and save people.

Having been born in this world,

the one thing man must do is become Truth.

He who has accomplished this

is a person who has accomplished all.

Only those who have been born and live as Truth

will be born as God.

Those who dwell in this world will live in this world,

and those who are born in heaven will live eternally in heaven.

The living can recognize both the living and the dead,

but the dead can recognize neither the living nor the dead.

Whether or not the green mountains and the clear streams -

the whole Earth - exist or disappear,

that which is born in the land of Truth does not disappear
because it is Truth.
Such is trueness.
The Savior, *Maitreya*, the holy person
you have been so eagerly waiting for,
the delusional entity that you are waiting for,
will not come no matter how long you wait.
But when the existence of Truth actually does come to the
    world,
in other words, when Truth itself comes to the world,
man must recognize that this existence is Truth.
He must listen to the words of Truth,
repent and be reborn in the land of Truth;
he must do the work of that land and live the life of Truth.
Such is the true way to receive or acquire blessings,
and those blessings are truly his own.

Blessings are not something that you can pray or beg for,
blessings must be worked at to accumulate.
Blessings that are built in the land of Truth
do not disappear but last forever.
Heaven is within you,
and you will live eternally
with those blessings you have built.
A fool who has a low level of consciousness

will build his fortune in his illusionary mind,

while a wise person whose level of consciousness is high

will build his fortune in his true mind.

Until the day when this Earth becomes as it is in heaven -

a place of one, and a kingdom that lives according to nature's

flow -

everyone will work together as one.

Only A Person Who Is Truth Can Give Birth To A True Person's Soul And Spirit

A pig gives birth to a piglet,

a rabbit gives birth to a rabbit,

and a sparrow can only give birth to a sparrow.

When an incomplete and false man gives birth,

an incomplete, false baby is born.

But when a complete, true person gives birth,

he gives birth to a true person.

If there is a complete person in the world,

he will enable incomplete man to be reborn

in the complete world of Truth

with the complete body and mind of Truth.

The origin of Truth is the true soul,

thus only the true soul itself, the origin, can enable one

to be born in the land of Truth as a true soul.

A true person gives birth to a person who is true.

The World Of The Master; The World Without Death

Along with the silently flowing years
my life silently ages.
There have been countless regrets and countless memories.
There was no rest amidst the countless words, agonies and
    anguish
but it was all simply a false dream.

Within the human world it is not possible to know
that living and dying is all a false dream;
it is only possible to know when one is born in the true world.
But no one does know,
because no one has been born in the true world.
Man lives in vain holding on to life
that flows by with the winds and flows by with the clouds,
and because he holds onto that life even after death,
he is falseness in a false world.
He does not know that it does not exist,
just as a dream does not exist.

A person who is born and lives in the world
knows the ways of the world.

Because he lives in the world, as the world,

he is free from the years that come and go,

and he just lives.

But people living in the human world

cannot see the living person.

The silently passing years do not exist for him

nor is there a life that he has lived,

so his is the mind of the world.

The master of the world has enabled

only those born in the true world within them -

those who have become the mind of the world -

to be born in the world.

Only the master of the world can enable one to know

the ways of the world, and the reason man lives and dies.

The world that I lived in, where I was the greatest,

was the world of the ghost;

it was death.

Only the world where the master lives

is the real world and Truth

and it is the world where I live.

All the many things that flow by,

pass by within me, in vain

yet in the world of the master, there is no death.

The world that is reborn within me is this land and this place;
it is the true world, the world of consciousness.
Heaven amongst heavens, the land of God,
the land of divinity are all within me,
and because this world is reborn within me,
the reborn world is the world of the master
and it is my world.

Will You Vanish Forever Or Live As An Immortal?

The river that flows leisurely without a sound
does not try to know where it is going;
it just flows.
It does not even have that mind,
thus it does not have the thought
that it is water.
Only man has a self,
has conflicts with others at every turn,
with countless minds of regrets and bitterness.
Man who lives in the shadow of the world
has many troubles and so many minds of blame.
He lives with resentment because the actual world
does not fit the world he has made,
and other people's minds are not like his.

So many things have silently come and gone in the world
but they just lived and went,
without trying to achieve or fulfill anything;
this is the way of the world and the law of nature.
In the world there are things in existence and non-existence,
but the original master does not have form;

its appearance is everything in existence.

So what is there to seek and what is there to achieve?

Living with universal order, as nature does,

and like nature, living as the water flows -

living without a sound then leaving,

living without regrets or bitterness then leaving -

is the way of the world and Truth.

Man has forsaken nature's flow, the providence of nature,

and struggles to live for himself only,

but he eventually dies, trapped within his own illusionary
world.

He who tries to achieve, fails.

Nature goes to the origin while living,

following the providence of nature.

Man lives with his own will;

he is unable to go back to the origin

and lives a life that vanishes.

Only for himself, he builds a house of his mind

and living only for himself thinking he will not die,

he ends up dying forever.

I wish people had wisdom.

The habit of having has become man's only habit,

and he lives trying only to have more.

Everything in the world -

the water, trees, wind and clouds -

follows nature and lives with the universal order of nature.

They live with surrender because unlike man,

they do not have the mind of shadows.

Their mind is the mind of the original form.

This mind does not have suffering, envy or jealousy.

Because it is without human minds,

and it is free from the countless different forms of greed,

it is a place of great freedom, the place of liberation;

it is a mind that can live freely.

The original master must allow one to be born in the land of
    the origin;

then he can live and become an immortal.

Only man lives in his self-made mind

and needs to erase his non-existent world.

The attachments, regrets, suffering and burden

have become his possessions,

and he lives thinking only what is his is right.

But they are just his preconceptions and habits,

and none of them exist; they do not exist in the world.

Man dies loaded down by shadows of the world.

Cast it all off and become the mind of the original foundation

because only when you are reborn in that land

can you become an eternally living immortal.

There is nothing of any use,

nor is there anything to have.

Everything one has, he possessed

because of his feelings of inferiority.

If one dies with nothing

by the hand of the devil of time that flows silently,

what use was it all?

What meaning did it have?

The meaning and purpose to living life

is casting off the life of this world, the world of a dream,

and eliminating even one's self,

so that one may live forever.

Some end up vanishing,

and some become eternally living immortals;

so is this not a miracle of miracles?

The Everlasting World

There are many things in the blue sky,

but the sky just exists silently.

Regardless of whether those things exist,

it is always the sky.

The true sky in the mind of the original foundation

is not blue; it has no color, smell or taste,

no feeling, nothing it sees or hears -

it is the place where everything has ceased;

a place beyond human conceptions and habits.

Man lives inside his mind of delusions

but when he changes his human mind

to the mind of the sky before the sky that is eternally alive,

he is able to truly live.

As an eternal immortal, he will live forever

in his mind that has become the world.

Dō is changing man's mind -

the mind of copied pictures -

to the mind of the sky that is Truth,

the sky before the sky, and *Jung* and *Shin*.

Man with his mind of false pictures

is ever trying to possess more,

trying to fill his mind of hunger with anything he can,

but it is always suffering and burdens that follow

when one adds to his mind.

Until now, in the age of incompletion,

man could not become complete,

because he only studied how to have more.

If he subtracts what is in his mind,

man returns to the sky before the sky - the mind of Truth.

When he becomes the mind of the sky,

he does not have human minds;

he no longer possesses the world of pictures,

and instead he has the true mind of the world.

On the day he is reborn in the true world

with the mind of that world, this place becomes heaven;

the place of the eternal sky.

He who is born in heaven while he is living

becomes a complete person.

When one is eternally without death,

it is completion.

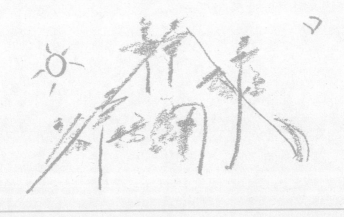

Part 5

The Living Empty Sky

This empty sky is the origin;

this empty sky is the mother and father of all creations in the Universe;

this empty sky is the master of all things in the Universe;

this empty sky itself is Truth.

All Of Creation

All creations are born from Truth, the original foundation,
and return to the original foundation.
They are alive,
because the original foundation is alive.
Everything has the lifespan of its form,
and its form itself is the image of the Creator -
the original foundation.
Everything that is material is born
and then disappears,
but what is reborn in the original foundation
does not ever disappear.

Truth And Falseness

Truth is what exists;

falseness is what does not exist.

Truth is what is living;

falseness is what is dead.

Truth is life;

falseness is an illusion without life.

Truth is everything in the world;

falseness is the human body and mind.

Truth is an eternal living existence;

falseness is an illusion, pictures, and not true.

Falseness is pictures taken of what belongs to the world;

Truth is the world.

Living A False Life

If you are alone in this unfamiliar foreign land
without relatives or friends,
there is nowhere to go and nothing to do.
And if you also had no money, nowhere to sleep or rest,
your life would be very bleak.
I had many dreams and aspirations in my youth,
but before I realized what I wanted to do and achieve
that time was gone.
Of the faintly lingering memories of the past,
not all of them are beautiful;
there were times that were desperate.
There was no one to take responsibility for my life,
no one who understood or acknowledged it.
The life I lived following my delusional dreams
was exhausting and with much toil.
I am getting old with the passage of time, and now
I am so thankful for all the difficult times in the past
that were my fated destiny.
I scolded myself often,
telling myself that I am not a great person,
or a clever one; that I am the one most lacking,

the worst person.

Most people live believing that they are great,

but I did not think there was anything great about myself,

nor did I tolerate deceiving myself in such a way.

In any case, time passed and I became Truth,

and I now see that in the dream-like life,

it does not matter how you live.

But because of my framework of mind, my preconceptions,

I made judgments of what I thought was right and wrong,

what was clean and dirty, cold and hot,

what I liked and disliked.

The mind of judgment had been my only mind.

In the lifetime of the human world,

there were many hills to climb, and many joys and sorrows;

they had existed because of my mind.

Even though one's life in the past

is an illusion that does not exist,

people live holding onto it in their hearts,

so they carry a lot of baggage.

Now that I am born in the world,

I know that I laughed and cried over my life, over nothing,

and I had put everything on the line for that life.

I regret having wasted years dreaming a false dream,

that has no meaning and does not exist in the world.

In the new world, there is no past and no future

and one sees the world as it is,

without even the mind of seeing.

The dream world that had been my life, has disappeared.

In heaven that until now we have only heard of,

there are no worries or anxieties,

and it is freedom and deliverance.

It is freedom because I do not exist,

and it is deliverance because I do not exist.

Because I do not exist, it is endlessly peaceful

and because I do not exist, I know God born in Truth is alive.

It is hard to know if I am awake or dreaming,

for I have become Truth

and now I know all the ways of the world,

that I had not even dreamt of knowing.

After erasing and eliminating my worthless self from the
    world,

only the world remains.

After discarding even the world, the empty sky remains.

When this existence itself became my mind,

I was reborn with the body and mind of the empty sky,

and I live as the Soul and Spirit of Truth.

My self from the past is false and my true self is real,

and the true world is within me and this place is heaven;

and my self born in this place will live together for eternity.

The master of this true land is he who has this place.

The time when one put everything on the line

for his false life has gone,

and I am thankful for all the unfulfilled dreams,

all the numerous things I left undone.

Everything looked for and pursued on the outside is false;

everything that is found within is true.

People all live the other way round,

and they only seek to gain from the outside.

The only true gain is what is gained from within;

only then can one truly gain or fulfill anything.

While each person has his own outlook on life,

his own set of values, he will know they are false

when his mind, of bubbles, is gone;

If he discards the bubbles,

he will also be able to know the ways of the world.

Water

The flowing water, even as it flows and flows,
always follows its path.
The water swirls and churns,
then becomes a cascade -
it is truly magnificent.
Flowing and flowing, crystal clear water flows.
Whatever is in its way,
it flows unhindered along its path
and even though it runs into thousands of things,
it flows without conflict, without speaking.

Following the flowing water's path,
descending valley after valley,
without change, the water is just water.
Water that is without minds,
goes and goes, somewhere, without any worries.
Even though many things happen,
because the water does not have the mind of those happenings,
they do not exist.
Whatever happens, it is silent.
It does not have even the mind of silence,

so it is free and liberated.

It is the always living Truth itself.

Water knows the laws of the original foundation;

it is the original foundation itself.

Whether or not water exists,

whatever it runs into,

whether or not this or that exists,

water that has no attachments to itself, is alive.

People, with their many happenings, with their many excuses,

with their individual minds, are shameful.

When one becomes the mind of the clear blue sky,

the mind of water, the mind of nature,

and is reborn from the original foundation,

only then, can one become

the divine, a saint, God, Buddha.

People, living with their evil sins,

do not know to be ashamed.

Believing they are superior and worthy,

they think the world exists for them.

Let's Find It Within

The migratory birds that fly overhead
have no fixed destination,
but instinctively know where they need to go.
When they get there, they stay awhile then leave.
Some die along the way
and some fly to the Himalayas, the world's highest mountains,
then fly all the way back.
But even for these birds that look so free,
death is always waiting nearby.

A person who wanted to live following the drifting clouds,
had thoughts of living freely in a world without hindrances.
He longed to leave, without destination or obstacles,
but could not, because of his ties and possessions.
In this weary life, this meaningless life,
there would have been times when he wanted to die.
His stifled mind may have wondered
what he can do to be free.
Having countless thoughts of wanting to throw off
the shackles of one's life is the human mind,
but leaving one's wife and children

and running off to a mountain temple or a foreign country

is not the way to let go of attachments.

To do so is a manifestation of one's feelings of inferiority

that he himself is not aware of,

whether the reason is to escape from reality or something else.

People get divorced or commit suicide together

because reality does not suit them;

even though they do it all in their own interest

it ends in regrets and sorrow,

and finally it does not benefit them at all.

In hard times when it was difficult

to earn enough to eat and stay alive,

many husbands who left their wives and children

to earn money in Japan, went and never came back.

The women spent the years as young widows,

wondering and waiting for their husbands to return.

But after growing old,

their husbands returned with new wives and children,

or sent word that they had a new family

and could not come back.

The women's lost youth had long gone,

with only bitterness remaining.

People lived their lives with many stories and events,

but everything that happens is bitterness and sorrow.

Whether they came or went,

there was no true freedom;

there was no proper life.

Where can one go, where can one live,

to be free, to have the desire to live?

Do not try and find it outside of yourself -

throw and throw away your worthless mind,

eliminate and eliminate your worthless self,

and when your worthless self no longer exists,

it is true freedom,

and you can go where you need to go and live well.

If you live as one with the wordless mountains and streams,

as one with the wordless sky,

as one with the wordless world,

you will lack for nothing and it is freedom and liberation.

There is no freedom or happiness

while you look for it as a slave to your mind.

If you become one with the world's mind,

your false mind no longer exists,

and you will always be at rest.

This mind never changes

and since that mind has no comings or goings,

you no longer come and go;

you have freedom and liberation.

He who lives having discarded his worthless self

is God, Buddha and a saint,

and he who discards this worthless self

can go to heaven while living,

the heaven we have only heard of.

While he may wonder if it is real or a dream,

when he knows the place he is living is heaven,

life will be truly joyful.

Even though the blue sky does not speak,

it does all it needs to do;

the mountains and streams do not speak,

but they do all they need to do.

Only man talks a lot and thinks a lot

but does not do anything properly; such is human life.

I like the world because it does not speak,

but I do not like people who speak so much.

Do they speak any words

that are not boasts of how great they are?

What is there to miss and what is there to do,

when it is all a vain and futile dream?

Just as when one wakes from a dream,

he knows the dream is vain and futile

and no longer struggles within it,

the elimination of your worthless self

is the medicine to wake from the dream.

Do Not Dream

The many stories and events lost in history,
have all disappeared.
For themselves, the people of those times warred, trapped,
ensnared others for their own benefit,
they battled constantly for wealth and honor.
Those countless many lived only for a moment
and then disappeared from the world.
Gallant heroes, kings, vassals and peasants,
disappeared with the passing of their era, of their time.
They all lived as slaves to their own minds;
they tried to gain and attain things within their minds,
but were not able to attain or accomplish anything.
All died whilst dreaming a futile dream.
A flowing river does not speak but does all it needs to do;
the sky does not speak but does all it needs to do;
the earth does not speak but does all it needs to do;
nature does not speak but does all it needs to do,
and lives for the world.
People however, who are busy with many things to accomplish,
have not done one thing for the world.
nor are they able to live in the world,

and as slaves to the false things in their minds,

they finally die while dreaming a false dream.

May this be a lesson to people -

so ignorant of the tragedy of disappearing -

who disappear after persisting with their selves,

instead of trying to be like the world.

Only he who knows is distressed,

but no one knows nor understands his anxious heart,

while his heart burns.

Do not try to leave behind your name in the dream world,

instead, make sure you remain in the world,

as the only value of human existence lies in living eternally.

But as no one knows that the meaning of mankind is in living,

man is unable to escape from the contents of the dream,

while living inside the boundaries of that dream.

It is lamentable, so lamentable.

The dream world of man is a lifetime spanning a mere eighty
    years;

for one who disappears after having lived those years,

his life is like a dream he had dreamed.

He disappears like a dream, like a wisp of smoke,

and nothing remains.

Nothing has ever remained in the world.

To receive a human body,

there must be a precarious chain of one's ancestors;

from one generation to the next,

and from those ancestors to the next,

linked generation by generation through the ages from ancient
times,

until you finally come to exist.

Isn't your existence, therefore, a miracle of miracles?

It is now the season when you can live,

so let go of everything and come into this season.

To come into season

means to be saved and live

during the time when the master of the world

has come to the world to save people.

Is there any meaning if one does not live?

Is there anything that is more important than living?

Of the countless ages that have come and gone,

now is the season when people can live.

If one does not live now,

the opportunity to live disappears forever and ever.

Therefore, the truly great are those who live in this time -

he who lives in this time is one who is truly great -

while the base are those who cannot live.

Stop dreaming futile dreams, come to your senses,

and throw away the story of the dream and all that was
dreamt.

Waking up from the dream,

and living out in the real world is the proper way to live.

Water flows by and time flows by,

everything that exists flows by and disappears;

such is the principle of nature,

nature's flow.

But when that which should disappear does not disappear,

that is to live and to be alive.

Wake up from the dream;

do not dream;

do not die after wasting the years

doing futile things for useless matters.

In the dream you betrayed the master of the world,

you made your own world and tried to become the master

but you were only busy,

while suffering and burdened without freedom.

Wasn't it futile to live by the contents of a dream?

Apologize and repent to the master of the world,

for stealing and living with that which is his;

for dreaming a dream.

Though they are told to throw away the dream

and come back to the master's world,

to be reborn in the true world and eternally saved,

people just continue to dream.

Wander and wander, though they may,

in a false world, in a dream, there is nowhere to go,

and they bear the suffering and burden

of the dream world, an illusion.

The medicine to awaken from the dream has arrived -

eliminating the dream is to wake from it.

Then, it is a new world and a true one.

Take the medicine, take it,

please take the medicine.

Only he who has awoken is toiling,

anxiously waking those who are dreaming.

People still do not know anything,

but in the hopes that if there are many people

who take the medicine and reap the benefits,

many more will take it,

my only thought is to give out the medicine

and wake people from their dream.

Fleeting Human Life

All people have periods of happiness and unhappiness.

Even if a person has a family that other people envy,

there is unhappiness within it.

He may wish for whatever causing this unhappiness

to be resolved, but when it happens,

he wishes for something else.

Wishing for human happiness is a manifestation

of the sense of inferiority in one's mind.

Even if man achieves everything he wants,

he eventually dies, and the past is all a dream.

If man lives knowing the way to live forever,

he would know what he needs to do.

Man is an entity that does not know anything.

His only wish is to get or gain things that he wants,

but this wish is just an expression of his delusions.

Time flows by, and all those whose lives have come to an end

have disappeared from the world.

Everything they wanted to achieve were like dreams,

dreamt during a brief nap.

Those who only exist in their thoughts have vanished,

without having done or achieved anything.

Man does not know the ways of the world

because he is not born in the world,

and he has never been born in the world.

He does not know the principle

that he exists because the world exists.

He has made his own world

by copying the things in the world,

and he lives within this mind world,

ignorant of where he came from and where he will go.

He runs around, for the fulfillment of his satisfaction only,

but no one can turn back the tide of time.

Only God can give man birth in the world without time;

only God can give salvation.

Salvation is giving one birth in the world without time,

and allowing him to live there.

There, time does not exist

so there is no birth, death, aging or sickness,

and because time does not exist,

one is an eternal never-dying immortal.

Man cannot prevail over time;

only God can take man

to the world that has prevailed over time -

the world that is beyond time.

Blaming the world and time,

suffering and sadness,

aging, sickness, birth and death,

desires, anger and foolishness,

the five desires and seven sins;

these things all exist in human life - the world of sin,

but they do not exist in the true world - the world of God.

The World Is Wide And Human Life Is Limited

My adolescence and youth has slipped quietly away,
time has eaten it up.
Time, please give me back my youth,
that youth that went silently,
without having done anything.
I do not ask for the fleeting pleasure of being young again,
perhaps I ask because regret remains;
regret that the world is wide
and the time left to save the people of the world too short.
My strength is running out and I am getting old
but I have yet to widely spread my message in the world.
People are immature -
they do not know where to go
nor do they have any true knowledge;
they lack the deep dedication in their hearts to fulfill Truth,
so they need time.
Without having etched the existence of Truth
deeply into people's hearts,
and without having resurrected them in the true world,
growing old is the enemy.
I am trying to send these glad tidings

to those trapped inside their framework of minds,

but people are bound in their preconceptions and habits,

which is all they know.

However, slowly with the passage of time,

my will that is true, will be known here and there.

When people do not achieve what they are trying to achieve,

when their greed to possess more suffers setback,

and their feelings of inferiority are not assuaged,

this message might be heard.

Those who have lost much in the illusionary human world,

those who are poor in spirit and those who are ill,

may come into Truth earlier

while seeking something to benefit them.

When they think about what it is they have achieved

and what work they have done;

when their families, their fortune,

or they themselves break down,

they may come to their senses,

and begin to hear the words of Truth.

Just as the wealthy do not toil physically,

those who have a lot of false scraps in their minds

because of those false scraps,

are not able to hear the words of Truth.

With all human matters, what is fulfilled

depends on the amount of effort and dedication put in -

such is the law of cause and effect.

Time, time, do not pass,

do not pass.

Until the people of the world have shed their suffering,

and until people who die trapped inside their minds are saved,

time, do not pass.

Although this is the only thing that must be done in this
   limited human life,

the world is wide and my mind impatient.

The Lifetime Of Man, The Lifetime Of The True World

So many people have come and gone from the world,
then more come and are gone again,
but no one in the world knows
where they came from or go back to.

Man is born into the world
through his ties, his karmic connections,
and though he lives with these ties
no one knows why he was born
nor why he is alive.

The sky that does not speak knows
where man comes from,
where he will go,
and why he lives.

Man, who lives within time that flows by silently,
disappears along with time
and leaves no trace in the world.

If one asks the sky where man has gone,

if one becomes the sky,

he will know that man is an entity

that does not exist in the world.

He has died, he has disappeared,

and that is all.

If there is a place he has gone to, it is hell,

but hell is a non-existent world,

for it is a duplicate of the world that man has made.

It does not exist because it is a world of delusion.

Man lives a life of seventy to eighty years, then dies.

But if he becomes the sky that does not die,

if he is born and lives in that place,

he will not die.

What exists in the world, exists

but what does not exist in the world

are delusions that do not exist.

Heaven is in the world,

and paradise is also in the world.

The only existence in the world that lives forever

and does not die, is the empty sky.

People think the empty sky exists without meaning

but the empty sky is a living existence

and the parent of all creation.

This existence is the source of the world,

and this existence is the origin of the world,

and this existence is the original foundation of the world.

The only existence in the world that is Truth

is this existence.

Without being reborn as the substance of the empty sky,

in the empty sky that is the Universe and Truth,

there is no place where the word *eternity* applies.

The empty sky is not material

but it consists of a living Soul and Spirit.

It consists of *Jung* and *Shin*;

it is the existence of the Holy Father and Holy Spirit

and *Dharmakaya* and *Sambhogakaya*.

This land is heaven

and this land is paradise.

In the world, only this existence is eternal and alive.

If one wants to live a life of the world without death,

the only way is to be born in this world.

Do not look for heaven in false delusions;

a wise person seeks heaven within the existing world.

From what I can see, the heaven everyone is seeking

is a false heaven of his delusions.

A Life Of Dreaming And The Empty Sky

A person who does not know where he should go,
where he is going, or which path to take,
is struggling to possess things in a dream.
He is busy but his busy activity is pointless.

One who has woken understands that the dream is futile
but he who is in the dream does not,
because he is still dreaming.
Although he is busily wandering around,
he is a false image wandering in his mind,
and he does not try to wake up from his dream
into the place of real Truth.

Life inside a dream is a life of pain and burden;
life inside a dream is an illusion;
life inside a dream is just a useless dream.
There are those who enjoy the dream
and ask to be left dreaming,
and there are those who inside a useless delusion,
agonize, moan and suffer, but either way,
those minds are theirs and not the world's,

so again, it is a dream.

When one's silent delusions have become his self,

he may move busily,

but anything he busily achieves is just a dream.

Like the silently passing time and lives in the world,

countless stories, events, this and that,

all become dreams and disappear, just as dreams disappear.

What one seeks or tries to achieve in the dream

are all dreams even if they are achieved or found.

The silent empty sky exists without a care

for the various stories of human life.

Only man dreaming a dream has many stories and events.

The silent empty sky creates all things, gives them life,

and lets them live with nature's flow.

People who go on and on about their lives

live trying to fulfill their will,

but once again, they are just dreams.

Unable to be one with the world

and live according to the world's will,

man who lives by his own will lives in a dream

because he has not been born in the world.

The minds of longings, regrets, desires,

good and bad, likes and dislikes;

the mind that discriminates

this is this and that is that;

they are all dreams.

None of this exists in the empty sky,

so it is complete freedom and liberation.

The empty sky exists beyond the human dream world.

Living without the mind that it is alive,

without words or any minds,

only the empty sky is noble.

It has no dreams or a life lived,

but it is alive; it is liberated.

This state of liberation is a place of holiness.

It is holy and supreme

because it does not have impure minds;

it does not belong to anything,

and it exists of and by itself.

It is holy because it does what it needs to do silently.

It is holy because it exists as an everlasting being

without the mind of having done all.

It is holy because even though it has no plan nor speaks,

it does all it needs to do according to nature's flow.
It is holy because it lives a life of nature's flow,
acts according to nature's flow,
and everything happens according to nature's flow.

It is holy because it does not have the mind
that something is hot, cold, dirty, ugly,
clean, good or bad, this or that.
It is holy because it has absolutely nothing.
It is holy because it has no mind to achieve
nor does it try to achieve.
It is holy because it has no greed at all.

It is holy because it does not have a care
whether the water flows or the wind blows,
or whatever events arise,
and because it is not within the hardships that come its way.

It is holy because it does not yield in any situation,
nor does it die, and it is free from all things.
It is holy because it is the master of the world,
the Creator of all things in the world,
without once showing a sign that it is so.

It is holy because it saves man and all things in the world

giving them all the necessary conditions to be saved,

and yet has no mind it is doing so.

It is holy because after having accomplished something,

it has no mind of accomplishment.

It is holy because after it has given all to the world,

it does not have the mind of having given.

It is holy because even though it created all material and
    spiritual things,

it does not have that mind.

It is holy because it saves and gives life to all things

without the mind or the plan of trying to do so.

It is holy because it saves all things in the world

without expecting anything in return.

Because it just does, it is holy.

An Island Journey During My Youth

In the middle of the vast ocean, the waves swell and surge -

it is impossible to know how far I've come

or how far there is left to go

but the boat pushes on, carrying me with it.

The waves are so strong,

the sound of the water slamming against the sides

shudders throughout the boat.

The thought occurs to me that we will die

if the waves overturn the boat

but the captain and crew go about their duties

as if all is normal.

The sea holds so many sad stories

yet it is silent, as if they had not happened.

In Korea, a country surrounded by water on three sides,

there are many widows whose husbands

lost their lives while fishing.

For them, the ocean must have been a sea of sorrow.

The wind blows without words,

and the sorrowful stories of those who lived by the sea

pass through my mind.

After a few hours, the pounding of the waves subsides

and a lone island comes into view.

From the bow of the boat

I can see villages scattered here and there.

Contrary to the lonely place I thought it would be

there are many villages, even in this faraway place.

The scenery of the rocky cliffs is magnificent,

and seeing them for the first time,

I stare at them in wonder.

Seagulls hover over the deep blue rolling sea,

it appears they nest in the rocky cliff face.

I arrive at the island and get off the boat.

Unlike the complicated people living in bustling cities

the people here are docile and without malice,

perhaps because they take after the mind of the sea,

the mind of the island.

To explore the island, I walk down a path

and along the way there are waterfalls and a steep mountain rise.

I walk with a group of female divers from *Jeju* Island

who have come all the way to this distant island to earn money.

Some are old, some are married,

and there are some who are single.

Since I am in my twenties

the younger ladies walk with me.

Perhaps because she does not want to dive anymore,

or perhaps because she dislikes the chilly sea water,

one brazen young lady earnestly begs me
to take her to Seoul.
Even though we have only known each other
for the length of the walk,
I see how blindly she longs to go to Seoul
and it seems she really dislikes her life as a diver,
always fighting against the waves.
There does not seem to be a weak diver
among the group walking in stoic silence;
without a word, they walk with ease.
As the sun begins to set, I climb mountain after mountain
and on the opposite shore from where my journey began
the ocean comes into sight.
I can see rocks jutting out of the sea
and a village with a town office.
There are many people living on this distant shore.
In the olden days,
the villagers would have used this mountain path
to get from place to place.
Here, when the fishing season is over
the men play cards and drink,
their lives passing with the sound of the waves.
The drinking houses are filled,
ringing with sounds of singing and drinking.
The waves pound against the rocks then shatter

just as they have done in the past,

coming and breaking, coming and breaking -

this is all they do.

But man lives his life as a slave to his own mind

and each has his own troubles and woes.

I decide to stay a night

in the only inn on the island.

The female divers are also staying here.

The diver who spoke to me knows I am here

but she ignores me and gets a room with her friends.

She stares at me blankly before closing the door to her room

perhaps because I had not replied to what she had said.

At the time I had no thought to respond

as I had come to the island to rest;

it was so far removed from what I had planned.

For the divers this place is their destination

but I carry on the next morning, after breakfast.

Along the seashore where the waves roll in and out,

alone, I walk and walk.

I see a house from time to time on the peak of the mountain

or built on a mid-cliff.

Perhaps there are other houses that cannot be seen,

hidden by the mountain.

Near the shore, there are places with a few houses

and areas with none.

On the way walking over the mountain alone

I come across a stranger.

I approach him cautiously and he too is cautious

but when I smile and greet him amiably

he responds with a friendly voice also.

After chatting awhile, I ask for directions

then we each go our separate ways.

I stop for some water at a shabby worn house in the mountains

and they tell me of their ancestors

who moved here from the mainland.

As I walk on I think of them.

The water flowing in the valley is so pristine -

pure snow melted into clean, icy cold water.

All the events in human life,

the stories of the people who live here,

as well as those who have come namelessly and gone,

remind me of the futility of life.

I leave the mountain and come to a village near the sea

and in a drinking house I ask for a bowl of *makgeolli*.

As I drink the hostess asks me,

Young man, where did you come from?

I answer her and ask which road to take, and then leave.

A little tipsy, I don't realize how tired I am

and walk on and on.

The seawater reflecting the sunlight sparkles

and the waves wash over the pebbles making them chatter softly.
Walking without purpose or meaning
I mull over human life -
living in vain in one place then passing away.
Alone, with my mind full of sorrow, I journey on.

The diver who wanted to go to Seoul in her youth,
must be a grandmother now,
or perhaps has already passed away.
Time flows by like a tale in a dream;
it was all a dream.

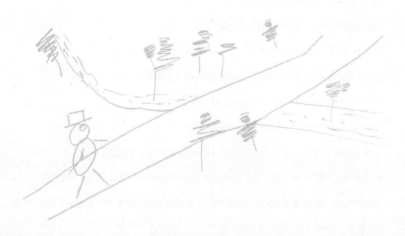

What One Came To The World To Do

Where are you going in such a hurry?
Why are you running wildly here and there?
You may regret the years that passed silently
but you cannot catch time,
nor can it be caught.
Even this moment cannot be caught
once it disappears.
You may hold onto what remains -
the mind engraved by those years -
but no trace of that time is left in the world.

Sitting by the flowing river,
I think about the futility of life.
Many who have sat and rested beside this river
have followed the years and disappeared.
Man lives out his one human lifetime,
inside the mind that he has made
but that mind is something that does not exist,
so he wastes his life; he spends it uselessly in a false world.
Yet there is not one person who wonders why he lives that way;
no one even thinks about it.

The new world, the land without minds,

existed from long ago, yet none have ever gone there;

it is a road far, far, from where man is able to go.

No matter how hard he tries, he cannot get there,

because man comes from a false world

that does not exist in the world.

Only when the master of the world comes,

that is, when a person of the world comes,

will he enable man to travel that distant path.

And yet, no one knows that it is the way of the world

that only when the master of the world comes as a human-being,

will man be able to go to the world,

and be born and live in the world.

If you ask the flowing water that aimlessly follows the river,

it is not interested in the least.

Nor are the skies or the trees in the mountains.

They just live a life of nature's flow,

following the principles of nature,

and they are free from curiosity.

They do not have human minds,

and therefore their mind is Truth.

True mind exists, yet it does not dwell within its existence.

It exists of and by itself,

free from minds and knowledge;

it is the mind where everything has ceased -

the mind of the emptiness.

It has no curiosity, questions or doubts;

and it does not try to know anything.

It does not see, hear, or speak;

it has no taste, sound or smell;

it has absolutely nothing.

This mind is the true mind;

everything in the world is born from this true mind

because this mind is alive.

If man had this true mind

he would most certainly have wisdom.

While it is the state of mind where everything has ceased,

it is also the mind that knows

the ways of heaven and earth,

the ways of the human world,

and the ways of the world.

Because God is wisdom itself,

God knows all through wisdom.

What one knows through words,

are words made within his mind, by his mind.

It is said that the origin of wisdom is knowing God,

because becoming one with God

allows one to know all the ways of the world.

Only he who has been absolved of all his sins,

with nothing remaining, can become Truth and know Truth.

If you do not exist,

only the origin remains,

you become the origin itself,

and the master of that land will enable you to be born in that
land.

While man dies after living seventy years within a dream,

he who is born in the world lives the life of the world,

and isn't the life of the world eternal?

If one is born with the soul of the world,

he becomes one with the world

and he is able to live in the world to the age of the world.

When man, from within his world of hell, the *saha* world,

destroys it, he is resurrected in the true world -

such is human completion,

and he goes to heaven while he is living.

Is there anything in the world more important than this?

Do not wander seeking something;

within you, there is God and Buddha,

and heaven is also within,

so when your mind of sins has been cleansed,

this land can be found within you.

Those Who Died Because The True Master Had Not Yet Come

Where should one go?
Where should one go?
Man who does not have a place to go cannot answer -
he does not know where to go.
Man who lives within false shadows
struggles within those shadows,
and does not know coming and going
or where to dwell.
In the many ages that have passed,
countless people have lived in this way.
Many pretended to be superior
with so many clever words,
but there was no true cleverness or superiority.
Man does not know anything,
and amongst so many that have been,
there was no one who truly knew;
no one has ever spoken words of knowing
or has ever taught others to know.

The place of knowing is the world,
and seen from that place, there was no one in the world.

He who has been to the world will know how to get there,

and he will know the ways of the world,

but the fact that there has been no path to the world

proves that there was no one there.

The countless many who spoke their own words

and not the words of the world, were speaking nonsense.

The reason there was no living person in the world

is a living person had not yet come to the human world.

A living person is he who lives in the world

and he who is born by himself must be the master of the world.

The master of the world had not yet come,

thus there was no one to take man to the world.

Only the master of the world can take man to the world

and enable him to live in his land.

In each religion, countless people are waiting for this existence

but those who do not have the world in their minds

cannot know even when this existence has come

or when he goes.

He who lives within his false world cannot see

as he does not have the world within him.

Man knows only as much as is in his mind

and he speaks and acts accordingly.

Thus in order to know the world,

the world must exist in his mind.

The Devil

The difference between God and the devil is:

God is love, great mercy, great compassion, virtue,

and nature's flow itself.

God just sees, just lives, and accepts everything.

God does not have minds.

God's mind is Truth, the non-existing mind itself.

God just lives.

God knows everything

and does not have the mind of discrimination.

Therefore it is the mind where all knowledge has ceased,

the mind that knows God's world through wisdom.

It is a mind uncluttered

by what the mind of the self has seen or heard.

Just as things are, just as they are seen,

it is freedom and liberation itself, of just seeing and just living.

The devil, which is not God, is the opposite of the above.

The devil makes predictions

and speaks as though he knows things.

The devil claims he is the best, and the king of Truth.

All of this is false; it is the devil.

The Definition Of A Person And A Ghost

He who lives in the world is a person, a true person.

He who does not live in the world is a non-existent illusion, a ghost.

A person is born and lives in the world

while a ghost is not born in the world.

There are no ghosts in the world:

a ghost does not live in the world

but in its mind it has a world copied of the true world,

and in this illusionary picture, it too lives as an illusionary picture.

So a ghost does not exist, although it may seem to exist,

for it does not live in the complete world

but lives instead in the land of pictures.

A Person Of The World Who Has Come To The Ghost World To Hunt Ghosts

Heaven and earth are life itself,

but there is no one who sees heaven and earth that are life,

nor is there anyone who knows what they are.

Everyone is trapped inside his own mind,

his mind that is not heaven and earth;

and he may be groaning with pain, but he is already dead.

He is in a world that does not exist,

a world of illusion.

God and man are one,

but God lives in the world,

whereas man is trapped in a picture and is dead.

So the difference between God and ghosts -

both much discussed topics -

is that of existence and non-existence.

In other words, a ghost that lives in the non-existing world does not exist

but living within its ghost world, it believes it exists.

Only the world exists,

so a person who is born in the world lives as long as the world does,

and he is truly alive.

Existence can be born into existence and live,

that is, one can be existent and live,

only when one is born in the world, in the land of God.

Ghosts of all sorts have been in frantic revolt,

since I came to the world of ghosts to hunt them.

They have been up to too much mischief

so they are unable to throw their illusionary worlds away.

A ghost knows the events and stories of its life are

meaningless,

not to mention, its life as a whole;

but it only knows how to possess falseness

and consequently thinks it can also possess Truth.

Truth can only be sought; it cannot be possessed.

Seeking Truth means eliminating the picture world,

which is the ghost world,

as well as one's self that is a ghost.

But the ghost lives thinking the picture world is real

and judges what is right or wrong

according to the fixed conceptions and habits of that world.

There is nothing of any use in this, so discard everything -

discard yourself, your spouse and children, and your fortune.

The only way to go and live in the eternal never-dying world

of Truth

is to discard everything without exception.

When God appears, ghosts vanish.

God drives away all the ghosts with his wisdom.

Only God can do this.

The heaven of eternal life that we have heard so much about

can only be attained after one discards and discards again.

In its meaningless life,

in its meaningless world,

the ghost blames this and that,

thinking he himself is the best

and that only he himself is right.

Now that God has appeared,

everything is revealed to be false and an illusion,

yet the ghost is shameless

and thinks he is deserving of such things.

Even though God has let the ghost,

who lives in the world that does not exist,

be born in the world of life that does exist,

it is not thankful.

Instead he only tries to regain the ghost world

he has already discarded.

Countless ghosts run away

because they do not want to discard.

The Living Empty Sky

The rain is falling silently;
the misty raindrops are like fog.

The sky is empty,
but at the same time, there are many things in it -
clouds and water,
oxygen, hydrogen, and carbon dioxide.

Even though the sky is empty,
it has the Earth, the sun,
the moon and the stars.

There are vacuums in the sky where only pure sky exists
and there are parts of the sky with many material things.
Even though all these things are in the sky
the sky embraces everything without a word.

This empty sky's original appearance is formless and shapeless
yet it consists of a body and mind.

The empty sky is the Creator

and through the coming together of things,
"this" exists because "that" exists.

The Creator is omnipotence itself.
From this oneness come a myriad of different forms,
and this oneness gathers everything back to itself.

Do not try to search within delusions;
The right way is to search from the existing world.

People think heaven is inside their delusional world
and they have a vague belief they will go to heaven,
but the heaven they believe in is a delusional heaven.
However no one in the world knows this.
One who is born into the real world is
he who has gone to heaven.

Oh people!
Learn the principles of the world and be born in heaven.
Man has lived through many ages
but the reason man has no wisdom
is he has never had the viewpoint
of the master of the world - God - who is wisdom;
trapped in his mind,
he has never been to the real world.

You cannot know the world however hard you try.

You will only know the world when you become the world.

It is because there is the sky

that the world exists and could be created.

It is because there is the sky

that the world, people and all creations could be created.

This empty sky is the origin;

this empty sky is the mother and father of all creations in the Universe;

this empty sky is the master of all things in the Universe;

this empty sky itself is Truth.

The world is alive because this empty sky is alive.

Everything in the world is a representation of this empty sky.

It is because the empty sky is alive

that the place where all things come from and return to

is this place, the empty sky.

Man must get rid of his world of sin completely while living.

The empty sky must become his mind,

and in the land of the original Soul and Spirit,

he must be born as his Soul and Spirit.

Only then is he a person who lives in the world,

who has achieved human completion.

God's Will

The waning crescent moon is drifting
as if it is being carried away by the clouds.
Since when, I do not know
but the people of old must have seen this moon
and they must have seen the sun in the sky as well.
The silently flowing water,
flows and flows until it merges with the sea
and they unite without conflict.
In the countless ages that have passed,
there have been countless joys and sorrows of people's greed;
greed that arose from feelings of inferiority.
They remain as stories all over the world;
these stories have become history,
and are too numerous to count.
In the silent passage of time
man cannot live as the flow of time.
He holds his stories in his heart
and is unable to be one with the world.
He struggles inside his dream to make his dreams come true
but along with the time that has passed
he too, has disappeared and is gone.

The life that is lived only in a dream
is a life of wandering, lost inside that dream
and just as it has always been,
people continue to dream dreams
without knowing when their dreams will come true.
Man is not able to be born and live in the true world;
he disappears after living the futile life of a dream.
This is why people of old said human life is the life of a weed;
a life of a bubble;
a life of a floating cloud;
a life of a mere dream;
a life that is a useless existence;
a life of a dayfly;
a life like smoke;
a life that does not, does not exist.
All people who have come and gone
lived their lives this way.
I see that no one has become one with the world;
no one has been born as Truth;
everyone is gone.

No one in the world can stem the passage of time
that flows without meaning or purpose.
Everyone vanishes along with time;
whatever exists all disappears.

One may wonder, if God is perfect and complete,

why he is allowing man to live with pain and burden;

why he is letting us live only to die.

While one may question and doubt,

those questions and doubts are only the thoughts of man.

The profound will of God was to make man only resemble
him;

to make man have greed for material possessions

by making him copy all things in God's kingdom.

This greed led man to multiply in vast numbers,

and propelled the development of human civilization.

This was in order to harvest as many people as possible

at a time when the human population is at its densest,

so that as many as possible can live in the kingdom of God.

If man had been created complete,

he would not have felt the need to have children

for he would not have had any greed,

and the human civilization would not have developed.

God creates all of creation;

therefore all creations must return to his bosom

and be reborn as his children -

then they are Truth and without death,

and can live eternally in the land of Truth.

If one repents and completely disappears from the world

only the origin, the original foundation, remains.

Then, if God resurrects him in the land of Truth,

the original foundation, he becomes an eternal immortal.

Now is the time,

along with the world, to become one that lives,

instead of living an empty, futile, cloud-like life.

There is nothing more important than everyone repenting

and coming into the land of Truth and living.

Do not blame the passing time, the world,

or anyone.

When one blames his useless self and discards his self

he will not blame time, the world, or others.

This is the way the world can become one,

and the way to go to heaven while living;

and those who have completely repented will live forever.

When one sees the world after being born in the true world

everything that exists is Truth,

everything he sees is Truth.

All things in the world live according to their shape and form

and when seen from the viewpoint of the world, all are one;

The source, the emptiness that is alive, is the master.

Existence is non-existence, non-existence is existence;

this is the source, the original foundation.

Thinking You Are Alive Is A Dream - Save Yourself Before You Are Devoured By The Devil Of Time

Rain is pouring down;
late April showers are hurrying spring in.
As the rain falls I look back on life -
it has all become dim memories.
All of it was futile, it was just a dream.
Everyone - those who loved me,
those who cherished me
and those who disliked me -
has scattered and disappeared somewhere.
What remains inside my mind
are pictures that my mind has held onto.
All those who lived in the world, within time that flows,
were busy and noisy while living,
and though they tried to fill their feelings of inferiority,
they were unsuccessful, and have vanished somewhere
with just their regrets and bitterness.

That we are living is just a nap-time dream.
Just as when we wake from a dream
we discover that it is not real but false,

it is so with human life.

While one might not know whether it is real or false

when he looks from within himself,

as one knows that a dream is a dream when he has woken,

when man's consciousness sees from outside himself,

from the origin, human life is something that does not exist.

Human life is lived inside a false dream,

lived according to that scripted dream.

Thus man does not know he has died even when he is dead

and even the thought that he is alive

does not exist in the world and is a dream.

Your mind is the path that you have walked,

producing a video of sorts:

Because you live inside that video

you are truly ignorant of the world.

The world is real,

and when you live in the real world

it is possible to know the ways of the world

and the will of the world.

But because you live inside your own world

having turned your back against the world

it is a dream without meaning or purpose,

far from the world.

The life that one lives is a false dream,
gaining false things which become meaningless and false.
Such is human life and the human world.
All people were born and lived without meaning or purpose
and have all gone to a false world after doing false deeds.
Is there anything more lamentable than this?

The world is the land of the skies.
The world is paradise.
The world is heaven.
This land is a place of oneness,
a land that exists.
The land that does not die but lives forever
is the land of Truth.
For a person who has cleansed his mind,
his mind becomes one with the mind of Truth
and is reborn within it,
and thus he is reborn, resurrected.
Wherever he is, wherever he lives
is heaven and Truth and therefore, alive.
As part of the world, he lives without death
in the land of that consciousness.

People! Don't waste even a single moment -
Stop living a false life, repent your sins,
and come out from within your mind world.
Let's go to the heaven we have only heard of
while we are still living.
Know that the silently passing time is the devil
that devours people without rhyme or reason.
Don't waste your time with false deeds
and come out into the world.
Life in this world is all a dream.
No matter how good your life is
or how happy you are in a dream,
what use is it if it is not real?
What meaning does it have?
Save yourself,
before you are devoured by the devil of time.
When you are born in the world without time,
the world where the devil of time does not exist,
neither time nor death exists.

Alcohol That Was My Companion

The friends of my youth, of long ago,

really loved to drink. I also drank like a fish.

After a glass or two, the countless thoughts and worries

boiling over in my head like a pot of porridge, would vanish.

Alcohol would sweep away those regrets and sorrows;

when I could not do what I wanted to,

when I found worldly matters hard going,

I lived through it all with alcohol as my companion.

I drank so much that my nose turned red -

a symptom of alcoholism.

When people met in those days,

it was common to go to a bar and have a drink.

After a few, the alcohol in me kept drinking.

Passing out is the drunkest you can get,

but perhaps because I always ate so much,

I did not get to that state often.

Many nights were spent pouring and drinking

until the early hours of the morning,

and it was bothersome to have to go to the bathroom often.

Although alcohol can be necessary in human affairs,

for many, it became a poison that killed them.

I had a high tolerance for alcohol,

so much so that I used to think, in the world

there was no one who had drunk more than I.

I had a strong head for alcohol and could hold my drink.

I think it is curious that I am still alive

after all that I have drunk.

I have not had a drink for more than a decade,

but when I first started teaching Truth, I drank a lot.

After I was enlightened,

I could not get drunk no matter how much I drank.

Alcohol had been my companion,

it had consoled my loneliness,

banished my agonies, and eased my sorrows.

Perhaps it assuaged the feelings of inferiority

that existed because of my mind.

Alcohol took some friends to the next world,

and my drinking buddies started to disappear.

I am by nature hard-working so even when teaching Truth,

I taught whole-heartedly and diligently,

and due to that diligence, Maum Meditation grew quickly.

Once in a while, I think about having a drink,

but rather than the alcohol itself

I think it is the atmosphere I miss -

the atmosphere where one could talk without barriers.

Sometimes I swept out all the events in my mind with alcohol,

and at times I drank and drank without rhyme or reason;

perhaps I drank because of the unsolved riddles in my mind;

why people are born into the world,

and why they die.

Even as I drank, I worked hard,

so I earned a lot of money and lived well.

Now all the questions in my mind have been answered,

and my sighs, my curiosity, even alcohol, have all vanished.

I have no sorrow or loneliness,

nothing to achieve, no friends, no alcohol,

and alone, I write and write.

I write and write calligraphy and prose,

and in order to teach people Truth in the easiest possible way,

I live writing, then writing some more.

I teach the world's most difficult subject -

the method to become complete,

and to save the world.

But people do not have much perseverance;

having lived for their selves only,

their consciousnesses are dead

and they live in a non-existent world.

I try to teach people at a level

appropriate to their endurance,

but I find that they sorely lack dedication

in this most important of matters: of life and death.
I put in a hundred times more effort in teaching
than people do in learning -
I dedicate all of my time.

Many People

The river's clear water flows from Canada,
following the river's every bend
all the way down to New York.
It has flowed through the ages without words.

In this clean river that meets the ocean,
there are many small fish,
and some big fish too.
But even the fish, living freely in this flowing river
live with the circumstances of their environment.
In New York, the financial center of the world
the river flows around Manhattan;
it is here that the river finally meets the sea.
Even this place, with its relatively short history,
holds a lot of sadness and regrets.
With many people coming and going from different countries,
Manhattan is hectic and busy, full of people walking hurriedly.
All people have work to do, but here,
people seem to be especially busy.
With the passing of time, many people who had trod
the streets of this city have vanished,

and even the buildings have aged.

The sky, the earth and the river are still in their places

throughout all the trials of this world,

but these people, with all they have to say

and their many stories, will one day disappear.

After much time has passed,

and even the river and land have disappeared,

the sky will still exist.

If everything that existed in the world becomes the sky

and has a Soul and Spirit in the land of the sky that just exists,

the rivers and the land will also exist eternally.

When these become your mind and are alive within your mind,

when your Soul and Spirit is born, there will be no death.

People should not live so busily;

the most urgent matter is to know this principle,

be born in this land, and become free of death.

This is the only thing that needs to be done.

But man who does not know the principles of the world

only goes about his work,

and does not try to know the principles of the world.

With a heavy heart, I see many people die.

The One Who Takes You To The Complete Land Is A Complete Person

Man has been pursuing human completion for a long time,

but he has never achieved completion

because a complete person did not exist.

It is also because despite his efforts to achieve completion

he is ignorant of the complete world,

for he lives in a world that is incomplete.

A complete person must come from the complete world,

if man is to become complete.

A complete person is he who can teach incomplete man

and take him to the complete land,

and only he can enable man to live in that land.

The world where man lives is a non-existent picture world;

so man too, is an illusionary picture

living in a land of pictures.

He does not know he is living in that picture world

because it overlaps the real world.

He makes that world his own,

and lives with the preconceptions and habits of that world.

He thinks that what is of his own world is true,

that what is of his own world is right,

and he knows only that which is in his own world.
Such things are all untrue, and are just pictures.
They are mere illusions.

A New Age

Now is the age of the new heaven and earth,
when heaven, earth and man are saved and live,
and the consciousness of the world reaches its peak -
an era when all religions are transcended.
It is the age of man, when man is the highest:
When heaven and earth exist in man, inside man's will,
and man lives as the master, accumulating blessings
and living within those blessings.
Each will become the master, a Buddha, a king, within himself.
He will become the master of the world and be without death,
without the heavy burden and pain of human affairs,
and without the judgment of good or bad, likes and dislikes.
The preconceptions and habits that man has,
are just his mind, his illusionary self,
but they do not exist in the world.

It is the age,
when one can go to heaven while he is living -
the heaven which until now he has only heard of;
when buddhas, saints and true people -
those beings we have only heard of -

come forth in great numbers;

when he who was dead inside his mind

becomes one who is living;

when resurrection and rebirth happens for man.

Until now, countless many have tried and failed to find
their true selves,

but now is the time, when anyone can find his true self and
become a saint.

Man was inside a dream and he was ignorant,

but it is now the age when he can know the ways of the world.

Now is the time

when all that has been spoken of is fulfilled;

when heaven and paradise we have dreamed of comes to pass.

A time when man no longer struggles to appease his feelings of
inferiority,

and all people in the world become one;

a time when there are no divisions between nations

and everyone is one;

a time when religion, philosophy and ideology become one

and saints live working for the betterment of others;

a time when the sky has become low and within reach,

and people live in the sky, no longer feel inferior

and lack for nothing.

In other words, it has become a time beyond human
    conceptions and behaviors;
a time of achieving completion when people do not die
    after death,
but live forever;
a time when this world and the world beyond are not
    separate but one;
a time of endless laughter;
a time when there are no songs of lamentation for the dead;
a time when man has wisdom and no thoughts or delusions,
a time when the world is a good place to live
because people are no longer foolish and work hard;
a time of the land of Buddha;
a time free of the seven emotions and five desires,
free from birth, aging, sickness and death;
a time when this place here on Earth is heaven;
a time of a humanitarian world living in harmony;
a time when all become one and live forever;
a time when one becomes God;
a time when one becomes Buddha;
a time when one lives with nature's flow;
A time without greed,
when no one thieves or robs
and people do not do each other harm.
In a time when we can live without the law,

we must discard the evil, selfish, human mind
and change it into the mind of God.
It is the time to live reborn in the land of God.

Conclusion

The material things that are in the world came from the original foundation and the place they return to is also the original foundation.

There is a Korean expression often used to describe somebody who is foolish or wretched, the literal translation of which is, "he who hasn't been born in the world; he who is useless in the world." What this expression actually means is that man is useless because he has not been born in the world and is therefore not alive.

Salvation is material things being born and living in the world as Truth. And such a time is the age of human completion. When God, Buddha, the kingdom of God, and paradise exist in man's mind, he will be born and live in the true world that never dies. This is human completion.

All religious scriptures have prophesied the coming of this time. People believe that these things will come about from within the religions they belong to, but when falseness is made to become Truth, it has already become such an age. When that which is false becomes real, it is this age, and when man's human mind changes to become the mind of God so that he is born in the true world that is the land God, it is already this age.

Until now, it was the age of incompletion; an age of continuously adding to one's mind. In the age of completion, man must subtract what is in his mind, and the more he subtracts, the more he will come to know. This is enlightenment. When one subtracts what is false, his mind becomes real and what the real existence comes to know is enlightenment. And if he continues to subtract in this fashion, he will reach completion.

The reason people have misinterpreted religious scriptures and do not understand the ways of the world is they live inside their minds. Their minds are illusions, pictures that do not exist, and they have not been born in the world. Therefore, there is nothing that they truly know.

Their minds that have turned against the world which is the master, their mind worlds that have copied the world, fundamentally do not have life. Hence, people who live within their minds are dead; they do not truly know anything and will eventually die in those illusionary worlds.

However, those who discard their mind worlds will be born and live in the world that is true. While living, they will be born and live in heaven which can only be achieved by subtracting their minds that are false. This is the only way to become complete. Unfortunately, people who are living in a false world are unaware that they are not actually alive; that they are dead. And those who are living in the living world will pity the lifelessness of those people.

The existence of God and Buddha is Truth. Only he who is reborn with the body and mind of God, Buddha and Truth will live forever, here in this place. This is ultimately the message behind every religion. If there is a place where this can be achieved, shouldn't we all go and save our lifeless selves?

In this age, when one can become Truth and complete by subtracting, shouldn't we all discard our false selves, become Truth and eternal, never-dying immortals? The age when Truth was just spoken of has come to an end; it is now the age when people can become complete. Let us discard and subtract our false selves and welcome the arrival of this age with joy.

Woo Myung

Maum Meditation Centers
Location and Contact Details

Please visit www.maum.org for a full list of addresses, phone and fax numbers,
as well as the locations and contact details of over 240 South Korean regional centers.

[South Korea]
Nonsan Main Center
82-41-731-1114

[U.S.A.]
AK
Anchorage
1-907-865-5954
CA
Berkeley
1-510-526-5121
Diamond Bar
1-909-861-6888
Irvine
1-949-502-5337
L.A. (Downtown)
1-213-484-9888
L.A. (Koreatown)
1-213-908-5151
Long Beach
1-562-900-5585
Orange
1-714-521-0325
San Diego
1-858-886-7363
San Fernando Valley
1-818-831-9888
San Francisco
1-650-301-3012
San Jose
1-408-615-0435
CO
Denver
1-303-481-8844

FL
Miami
1-954-379-6394
GA
Atlanta
1-678-683-4677
Smyrna
1-678-608-7271
HI
Honolulu
1-808-533-2875
IL
Lake Forest
1-847-574-6232
Lakeview
1-773-904-7933
Morton Grove
1-847-663-9776
Naperville
1-630-237-4166
MA
Boston
1-617-272-6358
MD
Ellicott City
1-410-730-6604
NC
Raleigh
1-919-771-3808
NJ
Palisades Park
1-201-592-9988

NV
Las Vegas
1-702-254-5484
NY
Manhattan
1-212-510-7052
Bayside
1-718-225-3472
Flushing
1-718-353-6678
Plainview
1-516-644-5231
PA
Elkins Park
1-215-366-1023
TX
Austin
1-512-585-6987
Dallas
1-469-522-1229
Houston
1-832-541-3523
Plano
1-972-599-1623
VA
Annandale
1-703-354-8071
Centreville
1-703-815-2075
WA
Federal Way
1-253-520-2080
Lynnwood
1-425-336-0754

[Argentina]
Almagro
54-11-4862-5691
Flores
54-11-4633-6598
Floresta
54-11-3533-7544

[Australia]
Sydney
61-2-9804-6340
Perth (Mandurah)
61-8-9586-2070
Perth (Vic Park)
61-8-9355-4114

[Brazil]
Brasilia
55-61-3877-7420
Sao Paulo
55-11-3326-0656
Lindoia
55-19-3824-5842

[Cambodia]
Phnom Pehn
855-78-901-434

[Canada]
Mississauga
1-289-232-3776
Montreal
1-514-507-7659

Toronto
1-416-730-1949
Vancouver
1-604-516-0709
Westside
1-604-267-9088

[Chile]
Santiago
56-2-813-9657

[Colombia]
Bogota
57-1-487-4680

[France]
Paris
33-1-4766-2997

[Germany]
Berlin
49-30-2100-5344

[Guatemala]
Guatemala City
502-2360-6081

[Hong Kong]
852-2572-0107

[Hungary]
Budapest
36-1-950-9974

[India]
Gurgaon
91-97178-63915

[Indonesia]
Tangerang
62-21-5421-1699

[Italy]
Genova
39-349-364-2607
Milano
39-2-3940-0932

[Japan]
Fukuoka
81-93-601-5102
Kyoto
81-75-708-2302
Osaka
81-6-6777-7312
Tokyo (Sendagi)
81-3-6277-9610
Tokyo (Shinjuku)
81-3-3356-1810
Yamagata
81-238-33-9271
Yokohama
81-45-228-9926

[Kazakhstan]
Almaty
7-727-273-1893

[Kenya]
Nairobi
254-20-520-3346

[Madagascar]
Antananarivo
261-34-9120-308

[Malaysia]
Johor Bahru
60-7-331-0146
Kuala Lumpur
60-3-4257-1482

[Mexico]
Mexico City
52-55-5533-3925
Tijuana
52-664-380-8109

[New Zealand]
Auckland
64-9-410-3131

[Paraguay]
Asuncion
595-21-234-237

[Philippines]
Manila
63-2-687-1294
Clark
63-45-624-7858

[Russia]
Moscow
7-495-331-0660

[Singapore]
Marine Parade
65-6440-0323
Tanjong Pagar
65-6222-4171

[South Africa]
Pretoria
27-12-991-4986

[Sweden]
Stockholm
46-76-804-6806

[Taiwan]
Taipei
886-989-763-445

[Thailand]
Bangkok
66-2-261-2570

[United Kingdom]
London
44-208-412-0134

[Vietnam]
Ho Chi Minh City
84-8-5412-4989